I0813609

WHAT NO ONE *Tells You* ABOUT MONEY

Let us not become weary in doing good, for at the proper time
we will reap a harvest if we do not give up.
–Galatians 6:9 NIV

WHAT NO ONE *Tells You* ABOUT MONEY

THE REAL KEY TO GETTING UNSTUCK FROM SOMEONE WHO'S BEEN THERE

JADE WARSHAW

Published by Ramsey Press, The Lampo Group, LLC
Franklin, Tennessee 37064

The names and other identifying facts of some individuals whose stories appear in this book have been changed to protect their privacy.

Editor: Mary-Kate Tucto
Cover Design: Kyle Hofmann
Photography: Seth Farmer
Interior Design: PerfecType, Nashville, TN

ISBN: 979-8-887821-37-5

Printed in the United States of America

25 26 27 28 29 VP 5 4 3 2 1

For Sam, Prince, Zia, and my little birdie who flew away.
I love you all more than you can ever know!

CONTENTS

FOREWORD BY DAVE RAMSEY

In the words of A. W. Tozer, I never trust a man who doesn't walk with a limp. The first time I met Jade Warshaw, I immediately saw a wonderful, quick smile, a lot of intelligence in her eyes, and a deep passion for what we do at Ramsey Solutions. It was only later that I learned the incredible story of what she and her husband, Sam, have walked through—the story that you're going to learn about in just a few pages. It's one of fight and grit and determination. Getting knocked down, getting up again, and taking another swing. I've been teaching people how to get out of debt for more than thirty years. Jade and Sam took those principles and completely transformed their life—so much so that, in 2022, Jade joined our team as a Ramsey Personality.

Now, every single day, she's working to spread that message of hope, to help other people find the freedom that she fought tooth and nail to reach. Because you don't forget the feeling of having so much debt that you can't breathe. I can hear it in people's voices when I talk to them, and so can Jade. My old pastor used to say that a man with experience is not at the mercy of a man with an opinion. Jade has the experience, she has the knowledge, and—after leading too many Financial Peace University classes to count—she's also seen this stuff work again and again as she and Sam walked with thousands of others on their journey to get out of debt and build wealth.

So when she is passionate on these pages or passionate on the stage or passionate on the air about getting someone out of debt, about helping the hurting, it's because she's been there, done that, and has all the T-shirts. And let me tell you, she doesn't hold anything back. Jade has an incredible "it" factor when presenting onstage, behind the mic on *The Ramsey Show*, and in print. Her energy, her authenticity, and her vulnerability are unmatched. This book will cause you to laugh and cry and change your life. Because that's what *she* has done—and because what she's going to teach you is different from any money book you've read before.

When I went broke, I had to go figure out a plan for how to handle money the right way—God's and Grandma's way—that turned into our 7 Baby Steps. Jade had the plan, but she had to figure out a whole other side of the equation. And to be honest, it's usually the tougher side. At Ramsey, we know that personal finance is 80 percent behavior and 20 percent head knowledge. So yes, we need to get the basic financial head knowledge figured out. Math has a place, but it's not our main obstacle on this course. The biggest problem with *my* money is the guy in the mirror. If I can get him to behave, he can be skinny *and* rich.

Larry Burkett said it this way: Personal financial problems are not really the problem—they're the symptom of something else going on. When I've made financial mistakes, I can usually trace them back to something negative in my habits or character that needed to be healed.

Sound familiar? Sometimes it's simple immaturity, sometimes it's a fear from childhood, sometimes it's a messed-up marriage, sometimes it's as serious as addiction. But whatever it is that drives us to buy things we can't afford with money we don't have to impress people we don't even like, that's the real problem. The debt is simply the symptom. The mismanagement, the chaos, the lack of a budget, the lack of discipline are the symptoms, not the real problem. And until you face that root problem, the symptoms may change, but they won't go away.

That's what Jade is going to walk you through: dealing with the underlying issues. The emotions, the beliefs, the mindsets that you've held onto that are holding you back. She's not just handing you an Advil for a sprained ankle here—she's taking you all the way through physical therapy. It's going to be uncomfortable at times, but I can promise you that you're going to walk away stronger. Ready to get after it. Ready to take control of your money, once and for all.

By doing the things in this book, Jade and Sam worked their way through not only a pile of debt but a brand-new marriage and the people in their mirror. They're heroes. And they want you to be the hero in your story. She'll show you how.

Buckle up. This is gonna be a good ride.

INTRODUCTION

Emotions

I recently got back from a Caribbean cruise. It was seven days of island-jumping from one paradise to another—filled with tropical breezes, live music, fellow passengers sporting sandals and cabana-wear, and tall, colorful drinks with little umbrellas peeking from the top. In essence, it was everything that comes to mind when you imagine a Caribbean cruise. Except this cruise was far from normal because every single passenger, upward of two thousand people, was debt-free. And they'd all gathered with a purpose: doing the world's largest Debt-Free Scream.

Now, a Debt-Free Scream is just what it sounds like. You count down three, two, one . . . and then yell, "*I'm debt-free!*" Picture Mel Gibson in *Braveheart* shouting *"Freedom!"* Rocky Balboa yelling "*Adrian!*" after his victory, or Stanley calling "*Stella!*" in *A Streetcar Named Desire.* (Okay, that last one's not exactly the same vibe, but you get the point.) These people were shouting from their core—from the depths of what they've sacrificed to make it to this point. Honestly, it was pretty spectacular. And pretty emotional.

I mean, take a minute to imagine what that feels like. A life without payments? Finally! No paycheck drama, no student loan frustrations, no crazy car note, no debt. Just . . . free? Did you imagine it? *Sheesh*, no wonder those folks were shouting! We're talking about some pretty radical accomplishments! All in all, that cruise was a full *week* of celebrating some of the biggest milestones a person can hit with money. Many had even paid off their houses, and just as many were actual millionaires. What an incredible thing to witness!

Only, I wasn't just there as a spectator. I was part of it. I was one of *those people.*

I was debt-free. I was a net-worth millionaire. And, plot twist, I was one of the hosts of this incredible cruise event!

There was an outdoor jogging track on Deck 4 that circled the entire vessel—and on that first day at sea, I decided to take a walk around the ship, which turned into a walk down memory lane. I was surrounded by water and my thoughts as I reflected on all it took to get to this incredible full-circle moment.

In all honesty, it felt surreal—like something that could only happen in a person's wildest dreams. Especially when you consider where I'd started with money eighteen years ago: in a complete and utter financial mess. I'll walk you through the whole story later, but just know that back then, something like this was nowhere near my radar. Back then, putting gas in the tank was a struggle—forget taking a vacation. Back then, buying instant oatmeal was a treat—forget treating myself to a nice dinner. Back then, it was all I could do to keep the bank account in the positive. Shoot, finding enough loose change to buy an iced coffee outright so I wouldn't overdraw our checking account was a well-developed skill! I was so stuck. Who could even conceive of being debt-free? In my mind, something that preposterous was only for "those people," and I certainly wasn't one of them.

But years later, here I was, on this cruise. Suffice to say, I was feeling some type of way. I was feeling all the feelings.

Blurred Lines

When my husband, Sam, and I first started the journey of getting our financial life on track, I was so busy trying to keep it together that I could hardly comprehend a life with no payments. You might be feeling the same way: so overwhelmed by money setbacks and frustrations that the idea of actually being debt-free sounds like some fictional fairy tale—not real life. Not something that could ever be a reality.

I felt the same way. We'd started working a financial plan and pretty quickly realized, *Dang, this is a lot easier said than done.* The truth is, I struggled. But at one point, I realized I was struggling because of something I hadn't accounted for in the math: me. How I feel. My emotions surrounding money, what I need to do with money, mistakes I've made with money, insecurities I feel about money, and the list goes on and on and on.

The raw and the real is this: Money is emotional. And I'm talking big, toddler-style, Oprah ugly cry, *Grey's Anatomy*-style emotions. Man, you will go through the wringer! And if you aren't prepared, it's enough to stop your money-managing streak cold in its tracks.

No one told me. And if you're reading this, I bet you didn't know either. But in the words of Kevin Hart: You gonna learn today.

Nothing's Gonna Stop Us Now

This book is not about a plan for your money. This book is not about why some plans for your money are better than other plans. This book is not a get-rich-quick, thirty-day turnaround money management system.

This book is about you. You and your emotions, your habits, your beliefs, your way of doing things, your background, your relationships—because all of those feed into your feelings about money. And the truth is, it's a lot. Managing your money has been hard. Shoot, I'm tired just writing about it. And if any of that rings true for you, chances are, you fall into one or more of the following categories:

- Perhaps back in the day, you tried financial plans and couldn't stick with them. Now, you're sick of financial plans and you're hoping this book is different. (It is.)
- Or maybe you know you need to get on some kind of plan with your money, but it already feels too overwhelming—and you're hoping this book will help. (It will.)
- Or you just started a financial plan for the first time and it feels like you're not making any real progress. You don't

want to quit, but you're wondering if a person like you can actually win with money. (You can.)

If you identified with any (or all) of the above, you're in the right place. You're likely frustrated, angry, scared, and ready to give up—a whole slew of emotions. But I have a feeling you're also really hoping this book will be the lifeline you need. Because if you're anything like I was, you may be starting to think, *Maybe it's not the plan . . . maybe it's me.* I've been exactly where you are. Fed up with my money, fed up with feeling like I can't do it, fed up with all of it.

In this book, we'll get to know each other well, because I'm opening the vault on stories I've never told anyone from my journey to debt freedom and beyond. In this book, I'm saying out loud what so many of us have kept bottled up inside—the things I wish someone had told me!

Trust me, by the time you've finished this book, you'll realize that big emotions are normal when it comes to making big changes with money, and you'll understand there's a clear path forward. We'll even talk through all the tactical stuff so you'll feel confident working though it all. By the time you've finished this book, you will not only feel validated that the struggle is indeed real, but you will also have unlocked the path to freedom that felt so out of reach before.

And finally, for the first time, you won't be stuck. Instead, you'll be freed to make progress, not excuses.

CHAPTER ONE

THE FIGHT OF MY LIFE

Started From the Bottom, Now We . . . Here?

The thing I remember most about the weirdest, worst, most mind-boggling five days of my entire life is the man who was running on the treadmill next to mine, completely naked.

It all started out normal enough. There I was, enjoying my customary run: a brisk four miles at a 6.4 pace on the gym treadmill. I was in my zone, deep into an episode of my favorite podcast.

That's when *he* walked into the gym. He was fully clothed in athleticwear with a backpack slung over one shoulder. It was after-hours, so the gym was quiet aside from me and my husband, Sam, who was using the weight-lifting machines.

When we'd arrived, it was virtually empty. I had my pick of the dozen or so treadmills lined up along a giant glass window, which acted more like a mirror at this time of night. I'd opted for the one farthest to the left. So you can imagine my surprise when the man who'd walked in chose the treadmill immediately next to mine.

Are you freaking kidding me right now? I thought, shaking my head.

It was dark outside, so that large window the treadmills were facing reflected the inside of the gym clearly. Too clearly. Because in that reflection, to my disbelief, I saw the man standing at the base of his treadmill—right next to mine—begin to do the craziest thing. He began to remove his clothing, one desperately important layer at a time. Sandals, T-shirt, athletic pants, and then, to my shock and horror, his boxer briefs.

No, Lord! I thought. *Not the drawers!*

Despite the quiet of the gym, my mind was screaming, *What the h-e-double-hockey-sticks is happening?* But the ridiculousness taking place right before my eyes did not stop. As a matter of fact, it doubled down.

This man sat on the belt of the treadmill, pulled out a pair of running shoes, put them on his bare feet, and tied the laces tight. I watched in utter disbelief as he hopped up on that treadmill, set the pace for 6.0, and began to run.

A fully naked man. Running. Next to me. And to be perfectly, painfully clear, this man was not what I would call a "thirst trap." Far from it. With each rhythmic strike of his feet on the treadmill, my stomach lurched with disgust. The sheer insanity of it all was enough to make any normal person burst into laughter, tears, or flames of rage. Not sure which. Possibly all of them, all at once. Either way, I just wanted it to stop! Someone, make it stop!

You're probably asking, "Okay, Jade, why didn't you call the cops on this guy?" Or better yet: "Jade, I thought this was a book about making progress with money. Now all I have is this bothersome-yet-hilarious image that will live rent-free in my head—forever. Can you make this make sense, please?"

Fair questions.

To answer the first, Sam and I used to be entertainers on cruise ships, and on this particular trip, we very, *very* unexpectedly found ourselves working on a cruise chartered by a nudist community. No, we didn't know beforehand. Yes, I know you have more questions—I promise I'll come back to this.

As for why I'm sharing this bizarre moment of my life with *you* right now, in this book about how to work through the emotions and mindsets that are holding you back with your money, it's because this wild experience is a snapshot of a season in our life when we had to do that exact thing.

You see, just seven years ago, Sam and I finally finished climbing what we refer to as our Mount Everest of debt. We had painstakingly-yet-successfully paid off $460,066.56. Yes, you read that right—almost half a million dollars of debt. It took seven and a half years for us to climb that mountain. And it's the things we had to work through, both emotionally and tactically, while fighting to reach the summit that gave me the experience, empathy, and expertise that led me to write this book.

During that journey, it became clear to me that it's not just about finding a plan. We have to change our behavior with money. And it isn't a light switch. It's an emotional process. To truly change our behavior, we also have to work through the emotions that hit us when we look at our financial situations. If we don't, they'll hold us back and hold us down.

You may be there right now. Maybe you've struggled to get serious about a plan for your money. Maybe you've tried and quit. Or maybe you've never found the will to even get started! Whatever the case, I've been at the base of the mountain, just like you. I understand how it feels as you look up at that daunting climb ahead. But I'm here now to show you the way up. I'll tell you what to expect—the good, bad, and ugly—and what it takes to make it to the mountaintop.

How Did We Get Here? (Nobody's Supposed to Be Here)

Let's take it all the way back to May of 2007. Exactly two weeks after my college graduation, Sam and I got married. Neither of us had a big-boy or big-girl job yet. What we *did* have was a couple of music degrees and a shocking amount of student loans. Since the payments on those loans wouldn't start for *months*, we were focused on figuring out how to parlay our degrees into actual income.

As luck would have it, we were gifted a Caribbean cruise for our honeymoon, and inspiration struck as we watched all the wonderful shows night after night. We saw a pathway to careers in entertainment. So as soon as we got home, we got busy auditioning for various cruise lines.

It was during that audition process that I first began to feel the cracks in our finances.

We lived in Nashville, Tennessee at the time, and I needed to travel to Hollywood, Florida to audition for Royal Caribbean Cruise Line. I also needed to buy proper jazz shoes for the dance portion. All this required money—and our money was more than tight; we literally didn't have any to spare. Ahead of the audition, I remember rummaging through closets to figure out what we could sell to narrowly, and I mean *just barely*, cover the price of the dance shoes and gas needed to make the trip. I'm talking selling clothes at Plato's Closet and listing a busted-up Casio keyboard on Craigslist.

Thankfully, that resourcefulness paid off and Royal Caribbean hired both of us—Sam in the orchestra and me in the review cast of singers and dancers. We were about to make more money than I'd ever seen. Together, we'd be bringing in about $4,800 per month. Life was good, and 2007 felt like a win.

But in 2008, our entire life came crashing down on us.

Those student loans we'd been ignoring during the six-month grace period started to demand our attention. My payments kicked in late in 2007. Sam's hit in February of 2008, a month before we started our jobs on Royal Caribbean. We honestly hadn't talked about our money much before—because things *felt* financially okay—but we couldn't avoid it now.

That dream salary suddenly wasn't enough. It wasn't even close. We needed a plan if we were going to keep our heads above water. Our contract with Royal Caribbean was only for six months, and I wanted to make the most of it. Growing up, I'd always heard my dad say I needed a budget—so we thought, *Okay, let's do that.* We wrote out our income, about $4,000 per month after taxes, then we listed out the monthly payments we owed. This is what it looked like:

Monthly Debt Payments

Housing Payment

Mortgage $680

Car Payments

Hummer H3 $435
Jeep Liberty $303

Credit Card Minimum Payments

Guitar Center $59
Capital One $59
Firestone $50
Capital One $45
Bank of America $41
Victoria's Secret $34
Express $25
S&K $20

Student Loan Monthly Payments

ACS Ed Services (private) $730
Navient (federal) $623
American Education Services (private) $400
Nelnet (federal) $204
Navient (private) $84

I don't know if you've been tracking the math with me, but after all those debt payments were subtracted, we were left with only about $208. And this didn't even include other monthly bills like cell phone service—which we suspended so we could keep necessities like car insurance and HVAC in our townhome. We were on thin ice.

Sam and I realized that if we'd been "on land"—rather than on a ship where meals were covered, gas was nonexistent, and other daily expenses weren't an issue—we'd be deeply in the red, even while earning a "good" income. That $4,000 monthly take-home pay isn't what I'd call a lot of money, but it certainly isn't a little bit! Actually, it's close to the median American salary, which in 2023 was $59,384 a year, or around $4,200 a month after taxes, give or take.[1] The problem wasn't that we earned no money. It's that we weren't outearning the decisions we'd made.

We were the typical American household, going about our daily life, ignoring the impending doom of our finances simply because nothing had burned down yet. Up until this point, honestly, I'd been complacent. Indifferent. It was easy to hide from the fact that we were broke because the money always came from somewhere. But now the jig was up. This was the first time I felt true fear about our money situation.

There was no pretending things were hunky-dory. We were in trouble. A sobering fear slapped me across the face that day. It was the first time I had the distinctly uncomfortable feeling that we'd made bad decisions, and we would pay dearly for them.

Picture that scene from *Rocky III,* just before Rocky Balboa faces Clubber Lang in the ring. In an interview ahead of the match, the reporter asks Lang what his prediction is for the fight. He gives the camera an intense look, waits a dramatic beat, and hisses, "Pain."

Looking at the budget that day, I feared we were entering the ring for a financial fight. What I didn't realize is that this would be just the first in a long line of fights—all-out emotional brawls, really—that each threatened to deliver the KO. But I was right about one part: pain.

While I was being shaken out of my complacency, Sam was dealing with a whole different emotion. I didn't know it at the time, but he was grappling with guilt. Guilt that sometimes dipped into the deep well of shame. It caused him to shut down or get defensive at times. Because in his mind, the biggest bills seemed to be coming from "his side" of the equation. To be clear, *I* never looked at it that way, but Sam felt like he was the reason we were looking at this mountain of debt.

Going with the *Rocky III* reference again, Sam was a lot like Balboa after his trainer, Mickey, died: Sure, he continued training and fighting through the guilt and grief, but he didn't have the eye of the tiger—yet.

So once we saw the reality of the numbers, both of us did what any human would do. We tried to hide it! Minimize it, shove it in the closet, deal with it another time. And we did exactly that in the form of student loan forbearance. It seemed like a great solution at the time. Put those puppies on ice! Save those student loan payments for another day—another year! What we weren't savvy enough to understand is that those student loans still accrued interest. And even though payment wasn't due, we'd still *feel* the weight of what we owed each and every day.

In hiding from the problem, we were making things much worse—and we didn't even realize it.

We Need a Miracle

After that eye-opening experience with the budget, Sam and I had enough sense to knock out as many of our smallest debts as we could before our Royal Caribbean contract ended. And once we were back on land, we made some tough decisions. We needed to make some big changes to our lifestyle before our next contract started. And I mean *big*.

We decided to sell the tiny townhouse we'd been living in, which Sam and his mom had purchased years before, and move to Florida. The plan was to find an apartment with a month-to-month lease that we could let go when it was time to work on the ship.

Planning a move like that forced a new perspective on us. There's something about making a big move and packing up everything you own that causes you to really evaluate what you have. Do you like it enough to bring with you? Could you sell it? Was it worth buying in the first place?

As we loaded our life into moving boxes, it hit me that we had all this debt and not much to show for it except stress and payments. It didn't seem fair. After all, we'd done everything right—right? We'd done what culture told us to do. But now I could see what it had cost us.

> "Go to college to get ahead. Can't afford it? Get a student loan! . . . *You'll just delay having children and risk your marriage and sanity to pay it off.*"

> "You work hard. You *deserve* a new vehicle. . . *And we can give it to you for the low, low price of your financial future.*"

> "You're entitled to what you want, and a credit card can help you afford it. . . *Oh, and in the process, we'll steal your confidence to manage and live off your own actual money.*"

It became painfully clear that these "helpful" pieces of advice were straight-up lies. Because here's the truth: Student loans are a trap—Americans are ensnared in $1.63 trillion dollars as of 2025 (and that's just federal student loans).[2] The average car payment is between $523 and $735 a month—and more than 40 percent of Americans have car payments.[3] Meanwhile, close to that same percentage of adults feels unprepared financially for retirement.

Connection? I think yes.

And credit cards? Don't even get me started. Banks made $165.3 billion off credit card interest and fees alone in 2023.[4]

I realized I'd been played. That's when I got angry. Angry that I fell for the lies hook, line, and sinker. Angry that debt was setting us back. Angry that we were heading into *years* of major sacrifice. But if I was gonna be angry, then I was determined to use it as fuel.

That fuel drove the two of us to take what my pastor, David Hughes, calls a faith action step. It's a movement in the direction God has called you, often without knowing where the full journey will lead.

Sam and I believed that God desired debt freedom for us as much as, if not more than, we desired it for ourselves. After all, I'd seen Jesus' words written plainly in my Bible. "The thief's purpose is to steal and kill and destroy. My purpose is to give them a rich and satisfying life" (John 10:10 NLT).

Now I'm no Bible scholar, but I did understand this: At that moment, debt was our thief. It was trying to steal our joy, kill our brand-new marriage, and utterly destroy our financial future. God was offering a rich and satisfying life. Say less. If God told us to go to Florida—trust and believe we were going to Florida. Even if that meant attempting to sell our home in the middle of 2009—a little time period known as the Great Recession, when it felt like all hell was breaking loose around us.

Gas prices were skyrocketing, mortgages were being foreclosed on left and right, and the financial house of cards a lot of people had built was crashing down. And here came Sam and me, putting our townhouse on the market along with twenty-six other people in our community whose homes were identical to ours (or upgraded and better).

We needed a miracle.

But this was our faith action step. We loaded up the car and headed south. And I kid you not, less than two hours outside of Nashville, as we were driving along that curve on the interstate that shows off a beautiful view of the Cumberland Plateau, our real estate agent called and said we'd received an offer on our house for cash. Plus, the people wanted to buy all the furniture inside. (Since all that furniture was on a store credit card from Rooms-to-Go, this was especially juicy.)

The offer would allow us to pay off that credit card in full *and* break even on our townhouse. Nothing lost—which was almost unheard of in the 2009 housing market. If God is for us, who or what can be against us?

Now it was on and poppin'. That miracle gave us the confidence we needed to get straight-up stupid with this debt. As soon as Sam and I got to Florida, we decided to sell our Hummer. We were upside-down by $3,000, so we sold it and got a loan to cover the difference. That knocked out $24,446 (eliminating a monthly payment of $435). The $3,000 loan felt like light weight after that.

We quickly found an apartment and convinced the landlord to offer us a four-month lease until our cruise contract. We spent our last $600 on a tiny couch and table from Ikea, and an air mattress from Wal-Mart that would be easy to put into storage while we were on the ship.

We were committed to the plan now, and there was no looking back.

Over the course of our next two cruise contracts, we continued to make a good amount of progress on our debt. We learned and stayed motivated by listening to *The Dave Ramsey Show* podcast every day. But it still seemed like we were missing valuable information. I figured it wouldn't hurt to pick up a copy of Dave's book *The Total Money Makeover*. Once we were back on land, Sam and I headed to Barnes and Noble and decided we'd buy the workbook edition so that we could *really* dive in.

Total Eclipse of the Heart

Here I was thinking this book would simply motivate us and give us the next steps we needed. I had no idea what that workbook would actually do to me. As we filled in the blanks for debt totals, it felt like the room was spinning. Instead of showing us a light at the end of the tunnel, it felt like Sam and I were looking at an oncoming train.

It was the first time we'd really laid out the full picture of our numbers—including savings, bank accounts, and debt by *balance* (not just the monthly payments). All of it. There was nothing left to hide. And to be real, when I initially saw it all there in black and white, all the progress we'd made felt so small.

OUR TOTAL Debt

Capital One $ 59
Capital one $ 179
Express $ 308
Victoria's Secret $350
Chase $ 560
Capital one $ 564
S&K $ 582
Bank of America $ 1040
Firestone $ 1352
Rooms to go $ 1788
Chase $ 2052
Capital One $ 2078
Guitar Center $ 2,999
Capital one $ 2,854
Capital One $ 3,379
Sallie Mae $ 7992.25
Sallie Mae $ 10,000

Nelnet $ 11,498.77
Carmax $ 14,926
Nelnet $ 18,137.54
Hummer $ 24,446
AES $ 36,851
Navient $ 71,937
Townhouse $ 115,000
ACS $ 128,934

TOTAL: $ 460,066.56

In that instant, I felt hopeless—a deep sense of self-pity and an overwhelming sorrow. What had we done? Was it too late? Had we messed up irrevocably? Up until this point, I'd not allowed my emotions to go there. I'm usually the upbeat person. My glass is all the way full. I rarely wallow. I seldom worry.

Someone had once told us we'd die with our debt, and for the first time, I found myself wondering if that would be true. After all, in our time listening to *The Dave Ramsey Show*, I'd never actually heard someone call in with as much debt as Sam and I had. We'd been working *so* hard, but our efforts suddenly felt like a tiny drop in a massive ocean. In that moment, I couldn't see the way out. I couldn't math it.

Were we really as serious about getting out of debt as we claimed we were? Sure, we were making sacrifices and gaining ground, but we were also still taking trips we couldn't afford, and credit cards were still a very real part of our lives. We were creating new problems as quickly as we were solving old ones. We were still complacent in a lot of areas—and that was holding us back.

My reality was flipped on its head. We had way more work to do than I first realized. Work that I was afraid might be impossible. Well, so be it. It was time to do the impossible.

That day with the workbook was like an ice bath. When you initially force yourself into the tub, you want to jump right back out. It's a punch in the face of freezing discomfort. It steals your breath. But pretty quickly, a numbness sets in. And once you get out of the bath, you realize it was all for your own good. The ache lessens. Now not only can you begin to recover, but you also get a jolt of energy.

And that's exactly what happened to us.

Sicko Mode

Survival is human nature—our bodies will do everything they can to stay alive. But as they say, only the strong survive. When it came to our debt versus our freedom, it was survival of the fittest, and I couldn't let my emotions get in the way of survival.

Was I fearful? Yes.

Did I feel a level of guilt? Absolutely.

Was I angry? All the freaking time! I was ready to fight like a junkyard dog.

Did I wrestle with pity and feeling bad about myself? Yeah.

Did I ever want to just give up? Of course! There were days I was worn slap out and wanted to give up. And I know Sam had these moments too.

It all existed together. The fight and the desire to just give up, the courage and the urge to run away—it was all true. The feelings were real, but I had to be in control of them.

I was like Balboa in *Rocky IV*. I'd lost enough, and I wanted vengeance. I was ready to knock out anything standing in my way. I was speeding down the road with Robert Tepper's "There's No Easy Way Out" blaring on the speaker. I was headed to Russia.

In 2010, it was go time. If Sam and I were going to survive this, if we were going to come out on the other side as victors and not victims, we needed to go straight-up ballistic on this debt. I started to come up with ideas for how we could go faster. And it would definitely require more faith action steps.

We began working for ourselves as entertainers. Sam and I had developed our own show. And it had the potential to pay four times more but required crazy amounts of travel—so much so that we decided we could save money by moving into a rental condo and taking on roommates. Usually when I tell people this, they hear the theme song from *Three's Company* in their head ("Come and knock on our door . . .") or envision the cast of *Friends* having a blast in a giant New York apartment. This was not that. This was survival. This brought our rent down to only $650 per month plus split utilities. Financially, it was perfect.

In that season, I also had the idea that would change the course of our finances and our lives. We were on the back deck of Oceania Cruises' *MS Marina* having dinner. There was a beautiful sunset, and I specifically remember we were eating shrimp cocktail (a perk of working on cruise ships). And as we enjoyed our dinner, it hit me.

"Even if we work fifty-two weeks a year, the maximum we could make is $153,000 unless we can do multiple ships a week, which isn't sustainable," I told Sam. "Even at that rate, it will take forever to pay off the rest of our debt. We have to find a way to duplicate ourselves. What if we start a talent agency?"

When I said that, Sam's face completely lit up at the possibility. This was it. This was the idea. This could set us free.

In those many hours of listening to *The Dave Ramsey Show*, we'd heard Dave talk about your shovel-to-hole ratio. Basically, if you've got a big ol' hole of debt, then you need a big ol' income shovel to help you fill it. And this new business idea looked like just the shovel we needed.

Now, getting our talent agency off the ground was no easy feat. But with a lot of hard work and grit, we got the thing up and running and profitable. Over time, that business did exactly what we hoped; it helped us demolish our debt faster than ever.

By 2015, we'd paid off all our credit cards and our car—yes, singular, since we'd stayed a one-car household after selling that Hummer. The only things left to tackle were the student loans. Unfortunately, they were still a big chunk. And even more unfortunate, the interest they'd been gaining from minimum payments caused the balances to balloon. We got lucky that the Obama Administration had just enacted a new cap, stating that student loans couldn't exceed 7 percent of a borrower's income. Now, we didn't use that as an excuse to dillydally on paying them off. Instead, we used it to keep our minimum payment lower so we could focus on throwing all the freed-up income at knocking out the smallest debts, one principal payment at a time.

We were really making progress—and our cruise-ship career had blossomed into something far more lucrative than it began. Sam and I were working more than thirty-five weeks each year, doing multiple gigs per week, while getting our talent agency off the ground. The cruise lines flew us all over the world to join their ships in exotic locations, so there were parts that felt super glamorous—like shrimp cocktail at sunset—but on the flip side, the travel was incredibly grueling at times. However, by then we were doing whatever it took to make the income we needed to hit our budget goals. We were locked in on becoming debt-free and had a no-holds-barred attitude to get there.

So, it was nothing strange when our agent sent a last-minute email to ask if we could perform on a ship sailing out of the Caribbean. Of course we sent a speedy acceptance and asked for the dates and cruise-line information. When it came through, Sam and I did a quick Google search of the cruise to see the itinerary and found no record of it. That was a little strange, but our agent assured us the show was still a go.

Right before boarding the ship, I did another quick search and found a clue. A charter company had booked the ship, and we would be entertaining a chartered group of passengers—a group called Bare Necessities.

At this point in our career, we'd performed for a lot of charters. Insurance groups, a Harley Davidson charter, a smooth jazz cruise, even a rave cruise. (Oh boy, do I have stories from the rave cruise!) But Bare Necessities? That was new. So I went a little deeper down the Google rabbit hole. Turns out, Bare Necessities is a nudist community. You read that right. I cannot make this stuff up. We were about to embark on a *five-day nude cruise.*

By the time I learned this, uh, *minor* detail, contracts were signed, the deal was done—we were committed. And to be 1,000 percent real with you, we wouldn't have canceled even if we could. We were in the zone when it came to paying off this debt. We had so much momentum going, and that trumped everything, including five of the most awkward days of my life.

So, ladies and gentlemen, that is how I found myself on *that* ship, on *that* treadmill, next to *that* naked man. Now that I can look back with humor rather than trauma, it was kind of symbolic in a weird way. Because even on a nude cruise, there were rules. People were *supposed* to wear clothes in the gym, but my guy decided to break the rules and run as his freest self.

I was doing the same (in a much less gross way). I chose to forego the rules culture had set about money and debt. Because I too wanted to be my freest self!

And I was also running, but this wasn't just about exercise. I was running for my life. Running for survival. Running for my financial freedom. And just like the man on the treadmill, I didn't care what people thought of me as I did it! It had finally clicked that I was in control of my financial situation and my actions with money. I had the power to change my life for the better—so who cares that this man was jogging in his birthday suit right next to me? Who cares that we'd put ourselves in perhaps one of the most uncomfortable scenarios of my entire life?

By this point in 2015, I *believed* that Sam and I could and would pay off every dime of that $460,066.56 of debt. It was going to happen. And when I believed it, my behavior reflected that, and *nothing* would be able to stop me. Not cultural pressure, not my emotions, not even a ship full of three thousand naked people.

We were finally fired up on hope and determination. We'd accepted that, although the financial woes in our life may not have been completely our fault, it was our responsibility to make it right. We'd come to the powerful realization that no one was coming to save us. We had to be our own heroes. And so do you.

This next round is yours to win—it's time to start the fight. In the words of Apollo Creed, "*Ding, ding.*"

The Final Countdown

From 2015 on, Sam and I hit our stride. Things were clicking. We'd figured out the mystery of how to budget and stick to it. And up until this point, we'd done every side hustle we could think of—dog training, website building, cupcake selling, teaching music lessons, remote call-service gigs—and made good money doing it. One summer, I even worked installing vinyl tint and letters on commercial vehicles. (Let's be honest, ten out of ten would *not* recommend that last one!) We'd worked so hard. Thankfully, our talent agency finally took off, and we were able to let all those crazy side hustles go.

By 2017, things were really going to the moon. We had just one debt left to go—a whopping $91,000 private student loan. We'd done every forbearance, deferment, and payment plan you could imagine on this thing, but every reprieve had run out. The minimum payment was coming due at a whopping $2,000 per month. But we were ready.

Around this time, we fortuitously signed a deal with a cruise line to do a big production project. The invoice was going to come in at $98,000—what Sam and I needed to knock out that loan and then some! But we weren't at the finish line yet.

Doing that production work was one of the hardest times of our life—and I've just told you about years of painstakingly chipping away at this debt. We were originally given a year to deliver the project. But early on, the cruise line moved up the deadline. Suddenly, we had just four months to finish our part.

The bulk of the work fell on Sam, and he worked like a psychopath to get things done. Day and night. Night and day. Pages and pages of horn charts and transcriptions. I came home from a gig one day, and as soon as I saw Sam at the door, I knew something was up. He looked absolutely haggard. He was spent. Nothing left. His eyes welled up with tears.

"Jade, I'm so tired," he sobbed.

It was like one of those moments in a movie when you grab the person by their shirt or slap them across the face to snap them out of it. I grabbed his shoulders and shook him, looking deep in his eyes.

"We're almost there," I said. "And once this debt is gone, it will be gone forever. Just a little bit further. We're almost there."

I talk to folks all the time who are tired. They feel weary. And they're ready to give up. When I talk to those folks, I think about that specific time in our life, and it reminds me of one of my favorite scriptures: "Let us not become weary in doing good, for at the proper time we will reap a harvest if we do not give up" (Galatians 6:9 NIV). Some versions say "if you don't faint."

And that's the caveat. You can't faint. You can't quit or tap out. Even though you may *feel* like you want to.

Weeks later, the day came. The work was done. The invoice paid out, and the money to buy our freedom hit the account. It was by far the most money I'd ever seen in our bank account. Sam took a screenshot.

"I just want proof that this is possible," he said.

Then we did what we'd waited seven and a half years to do: We paid our final debt.

October 25, 2017, was our Debt-Free Day. It's a holiday in our home, and it always will be. It's a day to celebrate doing what we were told was impossible. To quote one of my all-time favorite movies, *Field of Dreams*, we had heard the voice say, "Go the distance." And we did.

I think you've heard it too. You've heard that voice telling you to go the distance. But you got spooked by the implications for your life and all the emotions that go along with it. Because you know the truth—that it ain't always easy, it ain't always fun, and it will require more than you've probably ever given.

And I'll tell you a secret: The day we hit Send on that final payment, confetti didn't fly and there was no parade. Nobody jumped out of a cake, and the Blue Angels didn't zip across the sky in our honor. We danced around the house, shouted, "Thank you, Jesus!" and cried happy tears. In our home. Alone.

Yes, on the surface our financial situation was forever changed for the better—and that was a reason to a shout! But the biggest, most profound change was on the inside. Those years of fear and guilt, shame and pity and anger—oh man, the anger. It was like a morning fog that evaporates as the sun brings the warmth of the day. Those emotions just rose up and out of me. They just . . . lifted. I realized I was free to let it all go. I had been carrying all these emotions, holding them as a badge, as a chip on my shoulder, as my reason, and sometimes as my excuse. Somehow at the same time, they also served as fuel in my tank. As much as those emotions often tried to hold me back, they were also the emotions that triggered me into action.

If you're reading this book, you've likely run up against your own emotional barriers. Being stuck between a rock and a hard place with your money isn't easy. Deciding to move forward isn't easy either. It's not always as simple as flipping a light switch and charging forward unbothered by your feelings, misgivings, or nature.

We each have our own backstory to wrestle with. I know this book just started and you aren't sure what you will do. You're at the base of the mountain, looking up. And if there's one thing I could say to encourage you—if there's one thing I want you to hear from this side of debt freedom—it would be this: "Consider it pure joy, my brothers and sisters, whenever you face trials of many kinds, because you know that the testing of your faith produces perseverance. Let perseverance finish its work so that you may be mature and complete, not lacking anything" (James 1:2–4 NIV).

Those are some of my favorite words of wisdom from Scripture, and they reflect how I feel today: pure joy. I wouldn't trade this journey or the fight for anything because of what it created inside of me.

But back when I was standing in your shoes, I had no idea if I'd be able to muster the tenacity needed to win. The whole thing felt so overwhelming. It was hard to know if it would all be worth it because I'd never experienced the things I was reaching toward. And no one around me had either. I didn't know if it would be worth the sacrifice. You probably feel that way too.

Here's what I can tell you. It is *all* worth it. Indescribably so. And even if you're not sitting at rock bottom like Sam and I were, I'm telling you, embrace the journey. There is a massive treasure at the end—and I'm not just talking about money.

Listen, there are a *zillion* reasons to walk this journey out. Yes, you will see the fruit on the outside regarding your money. And I won't lie, the changes in your money hit different. It's wonderful to have this kind of freedom! But the realest reason to walk this journey out is what takes place on the inside.

You become an emotional superhero. You learn how to control your emotions instead of letting your emotions control you. You realize you are powerful—you are capable beyond what you could ever imagine—and that creates a well of confidence that no one can take from you. You can continue to draw from that well anytime you face a difficult situation, money-related or not. By our Debt-Free Day, I recognized this shift in myself.

Where I was once complacent, I now felt urgency and autonomy. I no longer needed to hide from hard truths.

Where I was once frustrated, I now felt confident and understood the virtue of patience.

Where I was once racked with guilt, I now felt unapologetic and bold.

Where I used to feel fear, I now felt secure for the first time ever—and eager to embrace change and opportunity.

Where I was once pitiful, I now felt powerful and filled with hope.

And where I was once so angry, I finally felt *peace*. I didn't need the anger anymore. Because anger is needed to fight injustice—and I'd gone out and gotten my justice. The only thing left in its wake was peace. The same transformation is waiting out there for you too.

The question is, are you willing to fight to get it?

CHAPTER TWO

THE THINGS WE DON'T TALK ABOUT

Baker Street

The first time I ever heard the unmistakable voice of Dave Ramsey on the radio was back in 2005. My older brother was enlisted in the US Marine Corps, and periodically he'd have to make the near two-hour drive east to the reserve station in Chattanooga, Tennessee. On this particular trip, I decided to ride with him. I was a sophomore in college, and the deal was, if I dropped him off, I could use his 1992 Cadillac DeVille as much as I needed until it was time to pick him up again. Say less.

We hopped in the car and took off toward the Cumberland Mountains. Not long into the drive, my brother hit the button on the dashboard that scans the radio stations. It'd play each station for about three seconds—long enough for you to decide if you want to choose it—then automatically flip to the next station.

About six stations in, a man's voice cut through the static of music and typical talk radio.

"That's the stupidest, most *dumb-butt* decision . . . "

That was enough to cause my brother to hit the dial and stop on that channel.

"You ever listen to this guy?" he asked.

"No," I said. "Who is it?"

My brother didn't answer the question—he just turned up the radio so I could listen.

For the next hour and a half, I listened to the most commentary and conversation I'd ever heard in my entire life on the topic of money. Everyday money stuff, not the complex jargon I usually associated with money talk. I heard questions from real people who called in from all over the country looking for advice—and answers from the host, an expert in personal finance. The guy's name was Dave Ramsey.

Now, at this point in my young life, I had no real interest in money. (Probably because I had none.) So I was mostly just entertained by Dave's dynamic with the callers. I also felt compelled by the subject matter because it was the first time I'd ever heard money discussed like this—with such openness, vulnerability, and ease. I felt like I was learning, whether I needed the information or not. I listened as Dave took calls from people in all kinds of situations.

A stay-at-home mom who'd just gotten divorced and didn't know how she was going to make it with partial custody of the kids.

A guy who inherited family land that was split up between him and his brothers. They wanted to sell. He didn't.

A middle-aged guy, married with a baby on the way, wondering if he and his wife should take out a loan to get a new minivan.

And a couple who called in to say that, after paying off forty-something-thousand dollars of debt, they were debt-free.

We listened to the show for the entire drive that day. And when it was time for me to drive back on my own, I found myself searching for the station again. The show was over, but days later, when I started the return trip to pick up my brother, I was so happy when I searched the stations and was able to catch this Dave guy again. *Yes!* I thought.

Listening to *The Dave Ramsey Show* made the drive fly by. I loved Dave's no-nonsense attitude, the fact that he wasn't perfectly polished in his way of talking, and that sometimes, he really let people have it. But by the end of the call, you still got the overwhelming sense that he really cared about the people calling in. The show wasn't about him. He truly wanted to help people. After that trip with my brother, it was years before I'd hear *The Dave Ramsey Show* again.

At the time, I had no idea that a seed had been planted. I had no idea how much that show would end up helping me. Or the impact it would have on Sam's and my life and money.

It wasn't until 2008 that it all came back to me—in the midst of one of our many troubled money conversations as a couple.

"Hey, there's this guy named Dave Ramsey on the radio," I said. "I actually think he can help us."

Now way back in 2008, podcasts were the new thing. You could download episodes right onto your phone—which was lucky for us because we were about to spend a lot of time at sea. Hearing other people's stories offered us hope, and that hope was absolutely addictive. So much so that Sam and I listened to every show. Three hours a day, five days a week, for more than seven years.

We *needed* it. We were trekking through a dry desert of debt, our backpacks heavy with the weight of our mistakes and regret. This show was the refreshing hydration we needed—an oasis with cool, crisp water for our souls. And unlike credit cards and other quick fixes, it wasn't a mirage. It was real. And it taught us exactly what we needed to do to get out of debt *and* build a strong financial foundation for the future.

It was by listening to *The Dave Ramsey Show* (now called *The Ramsey Show*) that we learned about a plan that could help us get in control of our money. I'd never heard anything like it, but I knew it was legit. I'd listened long enough to learn that Dave was the real deal. He'd walked through his own share of tough breaks when it came to money.

As a matter of fact, the whole plan was born out of the mistakes *he'd* made with money. Specifically, leveraging debt in real estate and having the banks call in his loans. This man went from millionaire status to bankrupt in a matter of months—then built it all back up again, the right way. And for decades, he's been sharing what he figured out during that journey.

Dave laid out the plan in a book called *The Total Money Makeover*, which sold millions of copies. The major takeaway from the book is a common-sense money plan called the 7 Baby Steps. Everything Dave was teaching on the radio was based on these Baby Steps, and it seemed like just what Sam and I needed. After all, if it was working for all the folks calling into the show, why couldn't it work for us? Spoiler alert: it did.

I think that's why, almost twelve years later, I jumped at the possibility to be part of *The Ramsey Show* when the opportunity presented itself. I knew firsthand how important one person's story could be to strengthen and encourage another person. Now I've been hosting the show alongside Dave and the other Ramsey Personalities since 2022. It's been my great honor to deliver that same hope to folks by helping them learn how to work the Baby Steps.

So here's what you need to know.

The 7 Baby Steps are a tactical approach to getting out of debt, saving money, and building wealth sustainably over time. In essence, it's a step-by-step plan to get control over your money and ultimately find financial peace. There are just seven of these "simple" steps:

Baby Step 1: Save $1,000 as a starter emergency fund.
Baby Step 2: Pay off all debt (except the house) using the Debt Snowball method.
Baby Step 3: Stack up three to six months of basic living expenses in a fully funded emergency fund.
Baby Step 4: Invest 15 percent of your household income in retirement.
Baby Step 5: Save for your kids' college fund.
Baby Step 6: Pay off your home early.
Baby Step 7: Build wealth and give.

Here's how most people experience seeing this plan for the first time. On the initial read, each step is a brief one-liner of advice that sounds like simple common sense. Most folks get so excited at the fact that there is finally an easy-to-understand financial plan. The prospect of taking control of your money gets you so fired up that you feel like you're actually in the movie *Remember the Titans*. You probably even catch yourself pounding your chest and yelling out, "Strong side!"

Initially, you feel like Superman. *Nothing can stop me now!*

Then you start to dig into what it actually takes to accomplish each step, and you realize, *Oh, wait. There's a lot that can stop me now.* You realize every step has a decent amount of nuance and requires a lot of behavioral modification. That's when the feelings creep in and the objections start.

"But Jade," you say. "Here's why that doesn't work for *me*."

I've heard it all before, talking with callers on *The Ramsey Show*. Truthfully, I thought most of it myself over the course of Sam's and my seven-and-a-half-year journey. Let me show you how it plays out.

Hit Me, Baby, One More Time

I'm about to give you a peek at some of the "how to" regarding the Baby Steps and the emotions they elicit—but if you want all the inside information, I suggest you read *The Total Money Makeover*. Or you could do what I did and start binge-watching *The Ramsey Show*.

Have you ever seen a movie or read a novel and thought it was amazing, only to find out there were other movies or books that came first? Kinda like having only seen *Men in Black 3*, and then someone puts you onto *Men in Black* and *Men in Black II*. Game changing. The first two are necessary to make the whole thing make more sense.

With that being said, I wanna let you in on a little secret.

What you probably didn't know is that there are two "steps" that come before the 7 Baby Steps. *Hold up! Wait a minute!* I know, I know—the 7 Baby Steps are like the financial "bible" for so many of us. So what I'm about to say might sound like I'm trying to add to the "scriptures." But calm down. I just wanna make sure you win and don't leave out two very important pieces of information to the plot.

If it makes you feel better, we can call them "pre-Baby Steps" or "Infant Steps" or even "stuff to do first" (that doesn't have much of a ring to it). I'll just call them what they are . . .

The Invisible Baby Step

This first precursor to the Baby Steps is invisible because it happens in your mind and in your emotions. You can't see it. It's simply a decision. You have to draw a line in the sand and decide, *I'm not borrowing money anymore.* Remember this saying: "You can't solve a problem while simultaneously creating it."

I learned this to be true the hard way. I thought I could pick and choose, whether it was the whole "good debt versus bad debt" argument, the "who could ever buy a car without a loan?" argument, or even the "I'm the exception to the risks of credit cards" argument. Been there, done it all, got the T-shirt, wore it out, and gave it to Goodwill.

Debt is the problem, and you have to cut it off at the source. Otherwise, you'll spend a lot of time being frustrated, taking two steps forward and one step back. I know this is unsettling, but for now, just let it marinate.

Baby Step Zero

The second precursor to the Baby Steps is what I and a lot of the folks I work with lovingly refer to as "Baby Step Zero"—the budget. I'm calling it Baby Step Zero because a budget *is* ground zero. It's the site where everything happens first. The budget is the foundation for every single thing you want to build with your money. I'm not exaggerating! Without a budget, the other Baby Steps won't hit right. So let me walk you through some budgeting basics.

First, the best way to budget is a method called zero-based budgeting. This means you plan for how you will spend every single dollar of your monthly income *before* the month begins. Now, zero-based budgeting does *not* mean you should end up with zero dollars in your bank account. That's the worst! If that's the case, something is wrong (a lesson I learned the hard way). When you make your budget, be sure to include a "cushion" so that there's always a little extra money in your account and you don't accidentally overdraw.

And keep in mind, this is not a one-and-done thing. The budget should be updated every month because every month has different needs. And if you're married, the budget should be a joint effort. No one person should carry all the weight or call all the shots. Both spouses must speak into and agree on the plan.

If you want to learn more about budgeting the right way, do yourself a massive favor and download the EveryDollar app. It makes this concept of zero-based budgeting, and even partnering with your spouse on the budget, so much easier. (It's the only budgeting app I use now—and what I wish Sam and I had back in the day!)

Baby Step 1: Save $1,000 as a starter emergency fund.

What That Really Means

It's time to go *crazy* to get this money. Sell anything you can. I once put a pair of used bathmats up for sale on Facebook Marketplace for $5—and someone actually bought them. The moral of the story? All things are possible. Make it happen.

And once you have the money, you want to keep it liquid and keep it separate from your everyday checking account—a traditional savings account or a high-yield savings account is perfect. You need to be able to get to it in the event of a real emergency (and sorry, the latest Jordans drop doesn't count).

If you have credit cards, now's the time to cut them up. You have cash now. Maybe not enough to make you feel all warm and cushy, but you can get by without the plastic if a true emergency pops up. And I have found that it causes me to slow down, get creative, and solve emergencies with cash instead of running to debt to save me.

The good news is, it takes most people thirty days or less to save $1,000—and it's only temporary. In Baby Step 3, we'll build this fund up to all it needs to be.

How You Might Feel

Fearful: Some folks feel anxiety off the charts at this stage because they already have *more* than $1,000 saved. It's their security blanket. And now I'm telling them to, basically, drain it. The thought of temporarily taking, say, $22,000 of savings down to $1,000 to pay off debt has them feeling some type of way.

Skeptical: Other people don't think it's really necessary. In their heads—sometimes even out loud—they scoff. *What will $1,000 do in a real emergency?* Since it's "not enough," or it's not a "real" emergency fund, they think, *Why not just keep a credit card? I can pay it off the next month.*

Frustrated: *I've never been good at saving,* this person thinks. *The moment I get it, I end up pulling it right back out for something else.*

Comforted: Fifty-one percent of Americans have less than $1,000 saved for emergencies—and 33 percent have zero saved.[5] So, some folks feel comfort at the idea of having $1,000 saved for the first time ever.

Baby Step 2: Pay off all debt (except the house) using the Debt Snowball method.

What That Really Means

Get comfortable with sacrifice. The truth is, 78 percent of people are living paycheck-to-paycheck.[6] And if you ever want to *stop* living paycheck-to-paycheck and actually build wealth, paying off debt is nonnegotiable.

In this step, you use all extra money, besides retirement savings, to pay off all your debt except your home using the Debt Snowball method. The Debt Snowball works by listing all your debts smallest to largest by balance—not by interest rate or monthly payment. Pay minimum payments on everything to keep bill collectors from blowing up your line (something I know a lot about), but put any and all extra money you have toward the smallest debt in order to pay it off fast. Each time you pay off a debt, it frees up more money to throw at the next-smallest debt.

The point is to move quickly, so your intensity level needs to be high. At Ramsey, we call it "going scorched earth"—meaning you're doing the most to get this done. How far you take this usually coincides with how much debt you have and how quickly you want to be free. So, if there are things you can sell to get out of debt faster, you should. And downgrading your cars is probably first on the list.

Now, Sam and I went hard in the paint. That meant living with roommates, selling our furniture, sleeping on an air mattress for years, and being a one-car family for a decade. For you, it could mean cutting out DoorDash, selling a vehicle, and picking up a side hustle. And yeah, side hustles are pretty much a requirement in Baby Step 2.

The good news is, the average person or family is debt-free in two years or less on this plan. Sometimes when situations are more extreme, like with Sam and me, things can take longer. That's okay too. As long as you're moving.

How You Might Feel

Afraid: When people see the sacrifice that it will entail to climb that mountain of debt, the discomfort alone deters them. They're fearful of all the ways this could upset their current, comfortable way of life.

Discouraged: Other people hear it and tell themselves, *This is impossible*. They feel completely overwhelmed at the idea of trying to pay off their debt, be it $20,000 or $200,000. They feel like it could only work for someone with a higher income or a better set of circumstances.

Impatient: In our society, we like things now. And for most of us, we feel an overarching impatience when we think of the time it may take to accomplish such a noble feat.

Confident: Some people hear the idea of using the Debt Snowball to pay off all consumer debt and think, *Game on!* These folks make it happen. They believe it's possible to use their current income to get it done in two years or less.

Baby Step 3: Stack up three to six months of basic living expenses in a fully funded emergency fund.

What That Really Means

I finally get to pay myself! This is where you go back to that $1,000 starter emergency fund and stack up three to six months' worth of basic expenses as a fully funded emergency fund.

Now, whether you choose three, four, five, or six months' worth depends on several factors you can weigh. Consider things like your health, how many income streams your household has, whether you're married or single, whether you have kids, etc. Once you know your goal amount, keep the same intensity you had from Baby Step 2. Remember, the faster you move, the more likely you are to stay motivated. Now that you don't have debt payments, you'll be able to save up your emergency fund faster than ever.

Just like your starter emergency fund, keep it liquid in that separate account I mentioned earlier. Never invest this money—you need to be able to get to this cash easily. Plus, you don't want to risk an investment going sideways and not having the cash when you need it. Think of it as insurance rather than an investment.

Remember, this is an *emergency* fund, and what qualifies as an emergency really matters. Otherwise, this money will be like the wind—here and gone in an instant. For something to qualify as an emergency, it needs to check all the following boxes:

1. Is this unexpected?
2. Is it necessary?
3. Is it urgent?

If a situation doesn't check all three boxes, your best bet is to cash-flow the expense with your income. But if one of those real emergencies comes around and you *do* have to dip into it, you'll pause whatever Baby Step you've moved to and focus on building this fund back up.

The good news is, now you officially have a solid "insurance policy"—your own personal warranty to keep you out of debt from here on out.

How You Might Feel

Stressed: I've heard from a lot of people who feel so traumatized from only having $1,000 in the bank back in Baby Step 1—or who feel fear based on the state of the world in general—that they've convinced themselves they can't feel safe until they have twelve months' worth of expenses saved.

Exhausted: Others (myself included) got worn slap out in Baby Step 2. So the idea of being intense *yet again* almost makes us mad. We want to live our life, buy a house, move on—but there's still more required? We feel tried! Someone should've told us that Baby Step 3 is tougher than it looks!

Insecure: If you haven't started walking the steps yet, Baby Step 3 can bring up a lot of insecurity. Maybe you've never even come close to having this kind of money in the bank. You think, *I'm that adult who has worked really hard but has nothing saved.* You wonder if people *really* accomplish this. You wonder if *you* can accomplish this.

Secure: Having six months' worth of expenses in the bank—in cash—puts you in the top 20 percent of Americans. And for the folks who drained their savings in Baby Step 2, building this fund back up feels like they're giving themselves room to breathe again.

Baby Step 4: Invest 15 percent of your household income in retirement.

What That Really Means

It's time to build wealth, baby! Baby Step 4 is when you can finally start to invest. Hallelujah! From here on out, you're going to contribute 15 percent of your gross (before tax) income every single month for retirement. The best place to start investing is your company's 401(k) or a Roth IRA.

If your company has a traditional 401(k) with a match, invest up to the match—and then put the rest of your 15 percent into a Roth IRA. (Get that free money in the match!) But if your company offers a Roth 401(k), you can start there and max it out, then move to a Roth IRA if you have money left to invest. I like Roth retirement accounts best because you pay the taxes up front. So down the road in retirement, you won't have to worry about paying taxes as you withdraw that money.

When it comes to choosing the investment funds inside your 401k, or IRA, it doesn't have to be complicated. We typically recommend you invest evenly across four types of growth stock mutual funds: growth and income (large cap), growth (medium cap), aggressive growth (small cap), and international (emerging markets). This mix helps you spread your investment across funds that have more stability and are considered lower risk—and those that have higher risk and the possibility of higher reward.

You should always do your due diligence before investing in anything so that you know what you're putting your money into.

Never invest in anything you don't understand just because "Jade said so."

The good news is, you can find pros who are ready to help you learn all about this stuff at ramseysolutions.com/retirement.

How You Might Feel

Intimidated: A lot of us feel out of our depth when it comes to thinking about retirement. Can I tell you a secret? I used to think investing was only for "those" people. I literally thought investing was only for older rich white guys. Back then I didn't know that someone like me even had access because it was never taught. Not to mention, there's a lot of lingo and jargon a lot of people don't understand, and we're worried about making a mistake and messing it all up. And when we don't understand the stock market, we can feel a lack of trust or fear in putting our hard-earned money in these investments.

Impatient: People high-key hate the fact that we tell them to wait until Baby Step 4 to invest. Many people feel like the time it takes to pay off debt and stock up the emergency fund causes them to miss out on time in the market or the free money of their company match. What it amounts to (and this is said with no shade) is that they feel like they're smarter than the plan.

Regretful: Outside of impatience, the emotion I probably hear about most with this topic is regret. I get it—I felt it. I regretted the fact that Sam and I couldn't invest for nearly a decade because we had to clean up our money mess before we could invest. I even felt scared that it would be too late.

Excited: Others are excited to get to this step. *Finally, I get to start building wealth!* Even if they paused their investing to do Baby Steps 1 through 3, this is by far the most they've ever invested—and that's exciting. They've paid off the past and are pumped to look at the possibilities ahead.

Baby Step 5: Save for your kids' college fund.

What That Really Means

We have the chance to make things different for the next generation by making sure they don't go into debt for education. Let me start by saying you don't have to pay in full for your kids' college to be a good parent. Paying for all, or even part, of your child's education is a privilege for the parent and the child, not some kind of entitlement thing. Truly, you don't *have* to offer to pay for college at all.

But as a parent, you *do* need to have clear communication early and often and create realistic expectations and a clear plan. It's your job to show them how to pay for college without debt. When I was in high school, my parents told me, "You better be smart and good at sports because you don't have a college fund, and we aren't taking out loans." As a result, I intentionally excelled at sports and applied for scholarships. I ended up being offered several full-ride scholarships for sports and academics.

Now there's no magic number or ratio when you get to Baby Step 5. Do the research on how much it would cost for your child to attend an affordable state school, then use a calculator to figure out how much you need to save and when you need to start. At Ramsey, we recommend saving that college fund in a 529 plan or education savings account (ESA).

A 529 plan is a great option—you can use it for education, kindergarten through university. And you can transfer the beneficiary as needed. Parents can even use a 529 to go back to school. Just keep in mind that 529s are different in each state, so do your research and avoid any prepaid plans. ESAs are similar, but have limits on contributions and income, so be mindful as you choose.

The good news is, no matter how you slice it, going to college debt-free gives your children an automatic financial leg up in life.

How You Might Feel

Hopeless: A lot of people feel like paying for college is unrealistic in today's economy. Impossible. We feel defeated just thinking about it. What if your kid wants to be a doctor or a lawyer? What if they're Ivy League smart? We feel like we need to keep debt as an option *just in case.*

Guilty: Others want to do education debt-free, but we believe it's too late. The kids are teenagers already, and we feel disappointed that we didn't start saving earlier. Or we beat ourselves up for how we spent money on other, now trivial things that *could* have gone toward education.

Optimistic: Some of us feel optimistic. We know about scholarships, we know our kids are smart and could earn some, and we feel ready. Or maybe you feel blessed, like Sam and me, because there was a grandparent who had the forethought and generosity to start funding your kid's college when you could not. (Thank you, Bubbie.)

Baby Step 6: Pay off your home early.

What That Really Means

The treat yo'self season is back in full effect. It's time to enjoy life! Only now, you know how to do so the right way—without debt and without sacrificing important financial milestones like paying off your mortgage early (which is exactly the focus of Baby Step 6).

Ramsey Solutions did the largest study of millionaires ever and found that 67 percent of them had paid-for houses. And for most Baby Steps millionaires (regular folks who have worked their way to millionaire status), their personal residence makes up about two-thirds of their net worth. It's a huge step in building wealth.

But let me clarify: You don't have to be balls to the wall on paying off your mortgage like you were with your other debt. You *do* need to be intentional about putting extra toward the principal with regularity. There's no magic ratio or amount to aim for here either. And it can change depending on your season of life. There were times when Sam and I paid $500 extra each month. Then there was a season where we doubled the payment each month. Then there were periods where we chilled on the mortgage in order to cash-flow other things, like home renovations.

The good news is, most people who work the Baby Steps pay off their house in seven to ten years. In a world where the average home loan spans thirty years, paying it off in a third of the time is a boss move—not to mention the thousands of dollars saved in interest payments.

How You Might Feel

Disbelief: This Baby Step gets a lot of skepticism. I hear it all the time. *Really? You're telling me I'll be able to pay off my entire mortgage in seven to ten years? Whatever you're smoking, I'll need some to get on board.* I get it! Some of us are just trying to make rent and keep food on the table. Baby Step 6, what? We can't hear it because it truly feels too painful to hope for something so big.

Unsure: Some people can't understand why anyone would pay off their home if they could use the extra money spent in payments to invest elsewhere.

Intrigued: Some people simply never considered paying off their mortgage early, if at all. Then they realize owning their home outright could be closer than they thought possible—and that feels enticing.

Ambitious: Forget intentionality, these folks want to stay intense! They're so pumped at the idea of being completely debt-free, they want to keep the pedal to the metal. Owning their home outright is a huge emotional driver, and they won't slow down until the job is done.

Baby Step 7: Build wealth and give.

What That Really Means

Finally, the time has come for you to rip your shirt off Hulk Hogan-style and shout with joy! You've made it! Now it's all about continuing to build wealth, being crazy generous, and enjoying the life of financial peace you've created.

Now that you've got retirement covered, college funded, and the house paid for, you can expand your investing horizon. If you have traditional investment funds you want to convert to Roth funds, this is the time to do it because you can handle the tax bill. If you have the itch to buy real estate, now's your chance to do it—just make sure you pay cash. If you want to set a little play money aside to invest in truly dumb stuff, like crypto or single stocks, I suppose you could. But treat it like gambling, and don't bet anything you can't afford to lose.

The good news is, Baby Step 7 is also when a lot of folks look up and realize they're net-worth millionaires. Simply put: What they own minus what they owe equals $1 million or more. This includes all assets: houses, cars, investment accounts, a business—all of it. Now that's what I'm talking about!

How You Might Feel

Restless: Surprisingly, some folks get an aimless feeling. For so long, they had a clear focus and goal in front of them. Now they aren't sure what to do next. Weirdly enough, amid all the joy, some folks feel a little lost and want a plan for what's next.

Content: For some, their lives don't change outwardly too much. You may never know they're millionaires, because this journey was never about anything flashy. They have a quiet sense of contentment and peace. They like the feeling of being generous anonymously.

Ecstatic: The overarching feelings for most people who make it here are peace, freedom, and accomplishment. They see nothing but possibility ahead. They're thinking, *I'm going to Europe, and I'm donating to St. Jude Children's Research Hospital, and this is the year I finally put in my pool!* These folks finally feel freed up and jazzed up to go *live* like no one else.

Hold The Line

Whew! You can see there's a lot involved here. It's not just a financial plan—there's a lot to come to terms with emotionally. Right now you probably feel a little like I did when I first read *The Total Money Makeover*. Like the room is spinning because you realize there's a lot of work to be done, and likely a lot of sacrifices yet to be made.

But here's the thing. The Baby Steps are a *proven* plan. And if you do the plan the way we teach it, *it works*. Most people finish Baby Steps 1 through 3 in three years or less. This is not theory. This is 10 million people reporting back, saying, "We did it—it works!"

No matter your socioeconomic background, no matter your race, no matter your gender or marital status—it'll work for you. And I'm gonna go ahead and go there. If in this moment you're looking at your life and thinking you're the exception because of the color of your skin, the area where you grew up, your education level, or any other station in life, I'm calling BS right now. The Baby Steps work, if *you* work them.

This is the plan Sam and I embraced to pay off almost half a million dollars of debt. And I don't know if you saw my face on the cover, but I'm a black female—historically one of the most marginalized, disrespected, underrepresented people groups in our country. And I don't freaking care. This book is about making progress, not excuses. Statistics don't define you. *You* define you.

So let the arguments go, I'll help you let the emotional hang-ups go, and let's get into making history in our family tree. Maybe you didn't come from money, but, baby, money can come from you. I'm proof. And I know I just came in hot. I'm not trying to be harsh. If I sound like a bully at times, just know I'm on your side. I don't want anything or anyone pushing you around when it comes to your money, not even your own thoughts or emotions.

Because all those feelings I called out earlier? They can cause us to question ourselves and our ability to do all of this. I've felt them myself, and I've heard them countless times from the folks I coach through webinars, social media, and *The Ramsey Show*. But it's the people who are able to work through these emotions who are successful.

I say "work through them" because these feelings are real. They don't just up and go away because you found a plan for your money in a book or on YouTube. The pathway to successfully working this plan is as much emotional as it is financial.

Jesus, Take the Wheel

The truth is, when you decide to embark on a plan with your money, a lot has to change. Your beliefs surrounding money have to change, and your behaviors with money most definitely have to change. And that's not easy! Throw all these natural emotions into the mix, and it's easy to go off track.

I like to think about it like this: If behavior is the car, belief is in the driver's seat, but emotions steer the wheel.

In other words, behavior is the vehicle that gets you where you want to go. Your beliefs are what drive you—they're the foot on the accelerator. But when you hit bumps on the road or see an unexpected curve, your emotions can cause you to jerk the wheel and get off course.

When it comes to your money, there's no doubt you will have to change behaviors. We outlined those pretty well in this chapter already. But new behavior gets no gas and will stop dead in its tracks if you don't have a belief. This is the outcome of making that Baby Step Zero decision: You now have the belief that life will be better with no debt. The belief that you deserve to exist without financial stress. The belief that the borrower *is* slave to the lender. The belief that you can be free.

Emotions, however, have the ability to steer your vehicle. They can be good or bad. Determination will help you stay the course, fear can lead you off track, anger can make you hit a tree—you get the idea.

In this book, we're going to focus on the emotions. Because we don't talk enough about how unchecked emotions have steered so many (including me) off course at times. You can have the belief and agree with the behavior because you know all the stats, but man, those emotions can really jack you up.

When an emotion crops up, threatening to stop you from working the Baby Steps, and you don't deal with it, that emotion goes from being a state of mind in the moment to a defining state of being that keeps you stuck. That's a problem.

Over the upcoming chapters, I want to validate that these emotions are real. They're normal. It's okay if a tough emotion is your state of mind for the moment. But you can learn how to keep it from becoming your state of being for the long term. In this book, I'll show you how to work through the emotions that threaten to take you off track along your Baby Steps journey.

It's time to get control of the wheel again.

CHAPTER THREE

DODGING THE TRUTH

Don't Stop 'Til You Get Enough

I have a six-year-old son and a four-year-old daughter, and the rule in our house is: if you want a snack from the cabinet, you need to show me the snack you chose before you eat it. This is especially the case on weekend mornings; the kids are usually up before us, and they tend to wake up hungry. So I tell them to show me whatever they get so I can approve it.

Well, one day I bought mini granola bars—there were probably twelve in the pack. And the next day, they were all missing, but no one had shown me this as their snack.

"Hey, bud, what happened to all those granola bars I bought?" I asked my son. "Did you eat them all?" He said no.

Now look, I'm the boy's mama. I knew immediately he wasn't telling the truth. But I didn't have proof, so I didn't press the issue. Several days later, while straightening his room, I found all the wrappers stuffed in the cushions of his chair. And not just granola bars—all sorts of snack and candy wrappers. It's safe to say, the truth betrayed him.

The truth always has a way of making itself known, even when you try to hide it. But here's the thing: it could have been so simple. Let's rewind.

"Hey bud, what happened to all those granola bars I bought?" I asked my son, to which he could have replied, "I ate them." I would've then taught him a lesson, he would've learned why it's not good to eat that much sugar in one sitting, and we would've moved on.

Such was not the case. Instead, it got worse for him. The longer he kept hiding it, the more wrappers piled up, and the more he felt inclined to hide. It's possible that the bigger the mess got, the more embarrassed or scared he became of what the consequence might be. But what I really think? I think the more the bars piled up, the more he got all the snacks he wanted, and the more he realized he could get away with it seemingly scot-free. Why not continue?

I ended up taking him up to his room and showing him the trail of trash under his bed and the stash of wrappers.

"Well, I found where all the granola bars went," I said with a *Boy, you better not lie to me anymore* tone. "Looks like you've had quite the wild time."

By this time, I was frustrated. Parents out there, you know. My tone and demeanor toward the situation had changed. Before, I was curious. Now, I was ready to dole out a consequence. He could have gotten a conversation and a teaching moment. Instead, he got no TV shows for the rest of the week. In the end, it wasn't really the snacks that got him in trouble; it was the fact that he'd been hiding his behavior for so long.

I reminded him that, hey, if you want a snack, no problem. But from now on, let's do it the right way, and the healthy way—by communicating. Hiding things is a red flag that what you're doing is probably a bad idea and an indicator that someone whose opinion you care about would probably disapprove. Otherwise, you wouldn't hide it! At the end of the day, intentionally hiding is a form of lying—and not just to others.

"Be careful about lies," my mom used to tell me. "If you lie to yourself long enough, you'll start to believe it."

The truth is, hiding is one of the many ways we dodge the truth of a situation. And a lot of us handle money issues like my son handled that granola bar evidence: sweeping them under the rug (or stuffing everything under the bed). That way, no one can see what a mess we've made. And as a cohost of *The Ramsey Show*, where I talk to folks who call in looking for help with their life and money, I've found that people usually fall into one of two camps:

1. The truth of their financial situation is starting to betray them, and they're ready to stop hiding and fix it.
2. The truth of their financial situation is starting to betray them, and they're having trouble recognizing that truth.

So I generally start the same line of questioning I did with my son: What happened to all the granola bars? (Or in this case, what happened to all the money?) Then, for the rest of the call, we tread through the trail of trash under the bed. We pull out and survey all the wrappers stuffed under the couch cushion so we can determine the damage and plan out the best course of action moving forward. I also try to teach people the right way, the *healthy* way, to handle their granola bars—I mean, their money—going forward.

If you fall into the first camp and you know it's time to stop hiding, you're open to solutions, and you're ready to make a change, great! You're already positioning yourself to win. It's like that old adage says: The first step to solving a problem is admitting there is a problem to solve. That doesn't necessarily make said problem *easy* to solve, so keep reading; there's more here to help winning with money become a little easier.

It's that second camp of people I need to call out. Now I don't mean to "take you to task," but you need a little more tough love to help you see the reality of your situation—the reality that it's not sustainable *and* the reality that you actually can change it. I know this because I was once just like you.

Maybe you read Sam's and my story in chapter 1 and said to yourself: "Man, what a story. Now *their* life was off the rails! . . . Wow, *they* needed to do a complete 180. What a comeback . . . Yeah, *they* needed those Baby Steps. But it will never be me. My situation is under control . . . I got this. I make a good income—in fact, I just got a raise. The only *bad* debt we have is a few credit cards. But our student loans and cars aren't really that big a deal. . . I'll probably do Baby Step 3 because extra savings sound good. But nah, I'm not dealing with all that debt."

Or maybe you read Sam's and my story and said to yourself: "Hey, I'm happy you were able to do it. But Jade, honey, these are *adult* steps. Ain't nothing 'baby' about paying off debt, Jade! It's too real out here. I'm just trying to survive in these streets, Jade. I'm living paycheck-to-paycheck just trying to keep lights on and food on the table, Jade. Maybe this is something I can aspire to when my situation changes. But you are not with me here in reality, Jade!"

Listen, I get it. I feel your pain. But the truth is: You are still hiding behind this idea that somehow your situation is different. In your mind, your money situation still lies in this gray area of "exceptions to the rule."

Look, no matter what you believe, a house on fire is a house on fire. Some folks know the house is on fire but don't believe there's a way to escape. So they stay in the house and burn. Others don't think anything is really on fire because they don't see the flames. But I guarantee—whoever you are—you've been smelling smoke. Here's what it smells like:

- When bill and payment notices come, you just shove them in a drawer.
- You're using your credit card more and more, and the balance is higher than usual.
- You put fun events like Christmas or vacation on credit cards.
- You utilize the student loan plan that makes your monthly payment as low as possible.
- If you (or your spouse) gets laid off, you're screwed.
- The mortgage payment is squeezing you, but you keep quiet because you fought to get this house.
- You aren't investing beyond your match, or at all.

- You have no money saved.
- You have two car payments.
- You're in a job you hate, but you need the money to keep up with payments.
- You needed someone to cosign your loan.
- You're staying in an unhealthy relationship for the financial benefit.
- You feel pressure from friends and family to overspend, but instead of fighting it, you just say yes.
- You'd be embarrassed if anyone saw your bank account.
- You'd be embarrassed if anyone saw your list of debts.
- You don't know the balance of all your debt.
- You're unbothered by the amount of debt you have.
- You use buy-now, pay-later. Regularly.
- Your credit score sucks.
- You wish you could afford to be a stay-at-home parent with the kids.
- You run to the restroom to check your bank balance at the restaurant.
- Little questions about your money and future keep you up some nights.
- You've said, "Money gives me anxiety."
- You avoid talking about money with your spouse.
- You tell little white lies (or big lies) about purchases.
- You overdraw your bank account regularly.
- You never fill your gas tank all the way up.
- The idea of cutting up your credit cards truly scares you.
- You feel attacked right now.

Can you smell the smoke? Instead of hiding, you need to open your eyes to the reality of your situation and move with a sense of urgency to get out of the burning house before it crumbles around you.

Dangerous

You might be thinking, *But Jade, a lot of those "smoke signals" are normal.* And true, a lot of those behaviors I listed above sound typical of the everyday person in America these days. Plenty of people have debt and don't know the total off the top of their head. Lots of folks would be scared if you told them to cut up their credit cards. Tons of couples hate talking about money.

You might even be thinking, *Hey, I fit a few of these. And I'm doing just fine!*

And there it is—two of the most dangerous words: "just fine." Hoping things stay just like "this." For a lot of folks, that means staying in a ton of debt but able to manage the monthly payments because they've got a pretty good income. As long as it's the standard stuff everyone has (car loan, student loans, credit cards that we *usually* pay off every month), we feel pretty good. And if our credit score is high? Oh yeah, everything's fine. Which brings me to the next way we dodge the truth: avoidance.

A long time ago, I heard someone say, the enemy of great is "just fine." And that's so true—if we let it be. It's this idea that "fine" is fine enough for us to get by, so why should we strive for "great"? When we settle for just fine, we're avoiding what it would take to make things great with our money.

We simply settle for fine because we can't be bothered to go and get great. We lack it because we don't want to embrace a stitch of discomfort in the short term to create a far more comfortable life in the long term. That's avoidance.

Someone who is okay with being "just fine" fails to look at the full picture and ends up sacrificing what they want most for what they want now. All because their financial choices haven't choked them out . . . yet. This is the hardest person to pull out of hiding because everything *seems* fine. That house fire I mentioned before? It's not raging yet. But the sparks are there, and it's just a matter of time until something catches. And it doesn't take much.

The wife gets pregnant and needs to stay home with the kids.

The White House Administration changes and federal student loans become due.

You get laid off from a job you've had for more than a decade.

AI starts messing with your career field, and it takes longer than you expected to find a new position.

That gradual lifestyle creep finally crept up on you in the form of higher car notes and bigger credit card bills.

You had a freak accident, and you'll be back to work in a few months, but disability isn't enough to cover everything in the meantime.

This is when that "Everything's fine!" default detachment begins to melt away. Like that first time Sam and I did the budget, and I realized we didn't earn enough to pay our basic bills—this is when reality hits. The reality that you're one normal life event away from disaster. The things I listed earlier are not abnormal catastrophes. They're things that happen at some point over the course of most peoples' lives. Forty percent of Americans have lost a job over the course of their working life.[7] And one out of four twenty-year-olds can expect to go on disability for at least a year before reaching retirement.[8] This is the data out there.

And look, I'm not trying to be scary or fatalistic. These are just facts that you *need* to be aware of. These are not reasons to freak out, but they are reasons to realize that "just fine" is *not* just fine. You have to be intentional—and you can't be intentional if you are too busy avoiding the truth.

Man in the Mirror

Signals exist in our lives to help with this. Whether it's a smoke detector beeping, the charge indicator on our smartphone changing from green to yellow, or simply our stomach growling to remind us we need to eat, these signals let us know when an area needs our attention—and that it's best not to hide from it, definitely don't avoid it, and certainly don't do this final way of dodging the truth. Please oh please, don't ignore it. Trust me, I know that's easier said than done. Take my least favorite of these signals for an example: The Check Engine light. The signal of inevitable, impending doom. Arguably the most diabolical symbol threatening to single-handedly destroy the entire car ownership experience.

Or maybe it's just an indicator light that is super helpful for maintaining the health of our vehicle. *Sheesh, drama much?*

Why is it that when that little admonishment lights up on the dashboard of our vehicle, we tend to ignore it? Why does it immediately incite the feeling of foreboding, that tangle of anxiety deep in our gut? Instead of understanding that it's a gentle reminder that there is work to be done if we want to keep driving safely, it feels like an attack for some reason. It's always when we least expect it—and the last thing we need to be dealing with. And rather than deal with it head on, we ignore it for as long as we can and secretly hope it will just go away on its own. *Maybe it isn't real,* we rationalize. *Maybe it was just a fluke.*

The truth is, ain't nobody got time for this! This is massively inconvenient. I have to take the car to the shop, and some guy with greasy hands is gonna give me a laundry list of all the things I need to fix. It messes with my schedule, it messes with my money—this is the worst.

But if we don't take it in, we could literally break down on the side of the road. And *that* reality is even worse. That will be even more uncomfortable.

Okay, time to take the car in and look under the hood.

Take a moment to look at the Check Engine light blinking in your own life. I'll give you a hint: It's likely on that page where I listed all the "smoke signals" when we were talking about our tendency to hide. Take some time to go back and highlight anything from that list that's going on in your situation—and if any concerns come to mind that aren't listed, go ahead and write them in. Once you're done, consider that a win. You are now officially *not* ignoring the light (and you're no longer hiding from the truth that this *is* a problem)! And that's a big deal, because that information will help us crack the code on what the underlying issue is.

At the auto shop, the mechanics have those diagnostic machines they can plug into your car, and the machine will spit out a code. The code determines how serious the issue is. The hope is that the code denotes a problem that's surface level and easy to fix. But more times than not, the code points to a deeper issue.

I can almost guarantee that the highlighted items on your list are directly tied to an emotion around your money that you need to address. Later in this book, we'll go through the most common emotions that are likely stopping you or slowing you down, and how you can begin to fix the issues. And just like those diagnostic codes, some will be easier, surface-level fixes, while others could be a deeper emotional struggle requiring more time and attention.

But the thing to remember is this: When we experience the Check Engine light, when things start blinking and smoking and we're wondering what's going on with our money and in our relationships surrounding money, we shouldn't ignore it. If we ignore it, it will likely become worse. And next thing you know, things break down financially. And you find yourself stuck on the side of the road. Instead, we should view that Check Engine light (the smoking behavior you highlighted) as the helpful warning it is and run a diagnostic.

The very definition of running a diagnostic is to go through and identify problems and examine symptoms. We have to search under the hood to find the deeper issue, and since we aren't vehicles—we're people—I'll quote Michael Jackson to make my point clear: It's time to start with "the man in the mirror."

Human Nature

Why is dodging the truth so easy? It's like breathing. Something about it is in our nature.

Think about it. Hiding, avoiding, and ignoring inconvenient truths and silly mistakes as a way to cope or shield ourselves from consequences and reality (albeit ineffectively) goes all the way back to the beginning of human existence. One choice by Eve technically started the whole thing. I'm talking about Eve from the Bible and the whole Garden of Eden fiasco.

We all know the story, right? Here are Adam and Eve, chillin' in paradise. They have access to everything they could ever possibly need—and God gives them one rule (in my own words): "Listen, don't eat the fruit on this tree; it's dangerous. Follow this one rule, and you're all good. If you don't, there will be consequences."

But of course, because people have free will and we all have the proclivity to be influenced by the voices we hear around us—good or bad, tranquil or toxic—any of us can allow the wrong voice to influence us. It starts with our emotions, then it creeps into our beliefs, and before we know it, our actions follow.

Eve let one of those negative voices influence her. It was the voice of the serpent! You remember the story. The snake slithers up to Eve and is like, "Look, if you don't eat this fruit, I'm telling you right now, you're missing out. I mean, did God *really* say you shouldn't eat it?"

From that moment, he's jacking with her emotional state. She is questioning herself and questioning God's motives. She starts experiencing FOMO, and before she knows it, she's ignoring what she knows to be true and she's making a bad choice. Plus, she brings her spouse on this emotional ride, like, "Yeah, I've been thinking, and I decided to eat the fruit—and you should too."

Before you know it, they've both eaten the fruit and completely played themselves, and they've jacked up their family tree. And to make matters worse, they then try to hide it. They try to cover up the results of their mistakes with fig leaves. *Fig leaves?* Come on. And then they try to avoid the One who could fix the whole dadgum thing—the Man upstairs. (Well, I guess He was technically in the garden with them.)

Think about this: Adam and Eve had *everything* they could ever need—the world was perfect. If it was that easy to make mistakes and fall into the trap of hiding, ignoring, and avoiding, in *literal paradise*, imagine how much easier it is in today's world to slip up, especially with our money. Just like Adam and Eve, we will make mistakes. Because to mess up is also human.

We won't always get it right. But instead of dodging the truth when we make a mistake with our money, we have to treat mistakes like research. If instead of burying our head in the sand, we assess what happened and why, then we can learn. Then we can adjust. And soon, we don't have a need to hide, avoid, or ignore anymore.

Now we can actually see the truth of our financial situation, and this frees us up to move on with the next steps in the journey—because we now realize we actually have a journey to take.

CHAPTER FOUR

MONEY IS AN EMOTIONAL JOURNEY

There Goes My Hero

I clearly remember the moment I looked in the mirror and thought, *We are too broke to even have children. We are too broke to raise a family.*

Sam and I had just joined a ship in French Polynesia, and although everything around me was a beautiful paradise, all I could see was that everything I ever *really* wanted out of life was on the line. The pressure made my heart start to pound. I got the choked feeling in my throat, and I felt heat behind my eyes as tears began to well up.

The realization of that truth felt so cold. So final.

See, early on in this journey, Sam and I made the choice that *if* we were going to have kids, we didn't want to do it until our debt was gone. (That was our personal decision.) And for years, I'd tried to convince myself I didn't even want children. *We're free spirits*, I'd rationalize. *I don't want to be tied down—I want to pursue being a musician. Kids will hold us back!*

Truthfully, that was only a mental diversion so that I didn't have to face the pain of reality. Making it feel like my choice, as opposed to an unintended consequence of those money choices we'd made, was a coping mechanism. But on that day, reality came like a battering ram. The truth is, I *did* want a family. I was ready for it then . . . but our financial life wasn't. And so, we were suffering the consequences. I was thirty years old, and we still had a couple hundred thousand dollars left to go.

As I stood staring in that mirror with tears spilling down my face, it hit me: If we ever wanted to have kids and bring them into a financially stable home like we'd planned, we were going to have to dig a bit deeper and make even more changes. And Sam and I were going to have to work together to do it.

Those tears? They were 20 percent sadness and 80 percent resolve.

Have you ever had that type of moment? A startling realization that your life isn't headed in the direction you thought it would be? Financially speaking, anyway. Have you ever had that sick feeling that you are nowhere near where you thought you "should be by now"? Have you ever had that moment where you think, *Dang, I'm in charge here. If I don't change the direction of my life, I'll never end up where I want to be*?

I think most of us, at some level, want to create a life that is "better" than how we grew up. And it's not to insult our childhood. That longing to improve on the past is just an instinct inside of us. I didn't want our future kids to feel the weight of any financial struggle. Sam didn't want anything to come between us having a healthy marriage and healthy relationships with our future children. So before we could have the family we dreamed of, getting to a level of financial health was imperative. All these dreams were riding on the choices we made next.

Let's be honest, "Mama" wasn't getting any younger—so Sam and I felt the weight of being on a literal biological clock to get our life and our money right. I can tell you firsthand that the moment when you stand in the mirror and realize that everything must change . . . *Bruh*. It's not fun.

There's the overwhelming guilt, shame, and regret from the bad choices that got us here. There's the anger—feeling pissed off at the world and frustrated with the feeling that life just isn't fair. I bet you've been there too. And if we're not careful, it's easy to start to feel sorry for ourselves. Before we know it, we're wallowing in self-pity and starting to view ourselves as the victim of a bad hand.

But if you can begin to muster just a bit of maturity—just a bit of mental self-control—and sit with these emotions long enough, you'll also begin to realize there's a certain power that lies in that moment of realization. If you sit with it long enough, the pit in your stomach turns to fire in your belly because you start to understand that *you* are in charge. No one else. Just you.

You start to realize that when you hit rock bottom, there's really no place to go but up. And how long you sit there at rock bottom before you decide to go "up" is really up to you. You start to realize you have the opportunity to turn this thing around. You start to realize you have the opportunity to become a hero. And that's pretty boss, right?

Right.

But there's no getting around the fact that changing your ways with money is an emotional process. It's a journey. It's not a light switch you can just simply flip. When I look back on our path of walking the Baby Steps, I see the epic emotional journey Sam and I had to walk through. Committing to a process isn't a one-and-done deal, where you just shake on it and move forward with success. That moment in the mirror wasn't the first time we had to make a choice to commit to the challenge, and it wasn't the last. It's a constant battle to *choose* to recommit—over and over again. Because situations and emotions pop up—over and over again. You're forced to choose whether to stick to your commitment and stay the path or give up and hightail it out of there.

Have you ever seen the Disney movie *Hercules*? "Herc" is in training to become a hero, and his training requires him to test his skills against all kinds of monsters and villains. At one point, he encounters a dragon-like beast: the hydra. Herc thinks he has it beat when he lops its head off with a sword. But just as he begins to celebrate his victory, *two* heads emerge where there had been one. Each time Hercules cuts off a head, the beast multiplies. Can you imagine how frustrating and emotional that must be? Each time you think you've won, you realize there's another battle waiting.

Just when you feel like you're done with debt and ready to move forward, an unforeseen and expensive emergency causes you to want to reach for that credit card again. Just when you get that $1,000 saved, the car breaks down. Just when you paid off that student loan, after the excitement wears off, your spouse suddenly seems uninterested in moving forward with paying off the car next.

The list goes on and on. The hits keep coming. There's always another head to chop off. But even though the process is emotional and tiring, it's entirely worth it. Because at the end of all that work, just like Hercules, you will defeat the beast. You will be a hero—as long as you're willing to show up to save the day.

Intentions

Every year, like clockwork, I get the notification on my calendar that I have my annual physical coming up. And it's not just the typical physical but all the preventative appointments that come with it. I visit the gynecologist, I have a mammogram, and soon, yes in just a few years, this will also include a colonoscopy. Pray for ya girl. (But we aren't there yet!)

The point is, I have decided that no matter how uncomfortable these appointments are, it's the right choice for me to show up for them. I have decided that I feel better when I take action and power over my health. I've decided that looking after my health with diligence and care is a big, beautiful way to love and respect myself and my family. I know my family's medical and health history, and so I use that knowledge to my benefit. Some of that history is great, and I can likely expect health in many areas just based on genetics. But some of it isn't so great, and I know where a history of cancer and diabetes exists, and so I choose to do all I can to keep those genetics from expressing their existence in my health.

This is true with everyone. We get to choose if we will monitor our health. We have this one life and this one body. We know this is the case, but when it comes to doctor appointments, most of us avoid them! Let's be real—we simply don't like going. Nobody really wants to step on a scale and have the number said *out loud* for everyone and their mama to overhear. (Plus, we all know that nurse's scale is like a camera—it always adds ten pounds. That's not fair!) Not to mention, they never capture your weight in optimal conditions. It's always fully dressed, with sneakers on, after we've had breakfast. I mean, come on, man! Now we're another five or ten pounds heavier. I'm convinced they want me to leave depressed forever about my weight.

And as if that's not enough, now I have to undress, put on a piece of paper that's open in the back, and let someone who is basically a stranger give me a once-over.

"How long have you had that mole? Has it changed shape or gotten larger?"

"Okay, get ready to feel a little pinch."

"Sorry if my hands are a little cold."

Ooh. I shudder even writing it. It's the worst!

Then there's the bloodwork. Which, let's be honest, is basically a list of everything that could possibly go wrong. (And they wonder why I come close to passing out almost every time.)

And then I have to wait a few painstaking days for a doctor to call and tell me the results. Or for the labs to upload to an app, leaving me to decipher and search online about all the ways I might die.

"So, Jade, you're telling me I'm supposed to feel . . . okay with all of this?"

Nope. I'm not telling you that you have to feel okay or enjoy it at all. What's to enjoy? A mammogram squeezing the life out of you? Or turning your head and coughing? I'm not telling you to feel okay, or not to feel uncomfortable, or even not to flat-out dread the experience. But I *am* telling you it's absolutely, unwaveringly necessary. And if you simply accept it for what it is—strange and uncomfortable—and not let your emotions get the better of you, then that's half the battle.

Now we can determine the best way to get healthy or maintain our health.

Say It Isn't So

That's where a lot of you are today. You're at the appointment. Because you're reading the book, you've embraced the uncomfortable to see what you need to do. To see what's keeping you from feeling financially healthy, what's keeping you mentally stagnant with your money, and what the best way is to get (or stay) healthy going forward.

Now it's time to decipher the labs. The results are in, and here's what we know:

- 6 in 10 US adults report that they worry about their finances daily, and 4 in 10 say they lose sleep over the state of their money.[9]

- Only 17 percent of US adults said they took a class on personal finance in high school.[10]
- 88 percent of US adults say they didn't feel prepared to handle money after graduating high school.[11]
- In one survey of US workers, 81 percent reported being worried about losing their job in 2025.[12]
- 46 percent of US adults reported some difficulty paying bills, and 1 in 3 Americans (32 percent) were late on a bill payment in the past ninety days.[13]
- 78 percent said that if their current paycheck were delayed by just one week, it would be difficult to meet their current financial obligations.[14]
- Only 23 percent of Americans say they live a debt-free lifestyle. Meaning that most folks are in debt for most of their adult life.[15]
- Two-thirds of Americans say they plan to work past age sixty-five—with one-third saying they plan to because it's their only option. They have to work in order to afford necessities.[16]

"Say it ain't so, Doc!"

Listen, I could keep going with the lab results, but I think you get the idea. This is not healthy, and it's no way to live. Something has got to change. We're stressed about our income, we're concerned about our jobs and financial stability, we feel anxious about the future, and we're winging it with our money because the truth is, we've never really been taught how to manage it by a professional.

But here's the thing. This is not necessarily how we present on the outside. On the outside, we keep the poker face on. We keep our pride intact. And we keep on keeping on the best we know how. Whether it's by avoiding talking about money with our spouse or continuing to swipe that credit card or telling ourselves that $20,000 in the bank is ours—even though we owe CarMax $40,000.

We're skinny fat! On the outside, we appear slim and fit in the same jeans we wore in college, but we aren't healthy on the inside. Our strict diet of McDonald's and Dr. Pepper has unsurprisingly started taking a toll on the inside. Those labs tell us what's really going on under the surface—the raw and the real. What's happening on the inside is the true picture. And what's happening on the inside inevitably begins to show on the outside. For better or worse.

Right now, most of you are thinking, *See, this is exactly why I don't like going to the doctor. All they tell me is what's wrong with me.*

Yep, and then they give you a list of changes to make to your diet and exercise habits . . . or lack thereof. Say, for instance, that your medical labs show high cholesterol, high blood pressure, and that you're on track to be pre-diabetic. Your doc will likely put you on medication to help with the symptoms—but he or she should also tell you that if you want to deal with the root cause and really get healthy, you'll need to lower your cholesterol by eating more plants, fruits, and leafy greens. You'll need to lower your blood pressure by cutting back on processed foods and reducing your salt intake. Deal with potential diabetes by cutting back on sugar. Focus on getting less processed, high-glycemic sugar and getting more complex, low-glycemic carbs, sprouted fiber, and whole foods.

To which most of us would dutifully reply, "Yes, Doc." "I hear ya, Doc." "Sure thing, Doc."

The truth is, you probably kind of knew you were in for it. You know deep down you could stand to eat healthier and exercise more. But as soon as we pull out of the parking lot of our primary-care physician, the Golden Arches call to us or, suddenly, our mouth waters for Sour Patch Kids—and our mind has already started the bargaining process. We've already begun convincing ourselves that while those medical symptoms the doc listed out sound scary, hey, we're still here. Alive and kicking, right? *How bad could it be? After all, Jeff at work has high cholesterol, and I saw him pound down a porterhouse just the other day! And didn't the doc say there was a pill or something I could take to disguise the symptoms?*

And before we know it, we're back to our same old routine. Living the crazy life, zero bleeps given . . . until the next year, when the doc lays out the same health issues but paints a clearer picture of what's at stake: "If you don't get this on track, you're at high risk for a heart attack."

We nod.

"Yeah, Doc."

"I hear ya, Doc."

"Fruits and veggies, Doc. Copy that."

But still, no changes are made. The lure of the cookies, cakes, and steaks keeps us at an emotional and behavioral standstill.

My Prerogative

The truth is that most of us are what my grandma would call "hardheaded." It's not until we've had the heart attack and are sitting in the recovery room that we've felt enough pain and are sick and tired—and scared—enough to really see the truth and change. Most of us need a catastrophe as a catalyst to transform.

Why is that? I'll tell you why.

Bruh, it's *emotional* to let go of the foods we love—most of which have been with us from childhood. It's comfort food, for crying out loud! It's emotional when we're told that foods we love and grew up eating are killing us. Back in the day, I would've fought anyone who tried to take Velveeta out of my life. Who cares if you think it's bad? I love Velveeta, and it's *my life! Humph!* (Crosses arms in stubbornness.)

I was ready and willing to stand on business. I'd defend my beloved Velveeta to the bitter end! Until, that is, I learned what Velveeta contains. Once I took the time to read about how processed cheese is made and what they do to it to make it sit on the shelf for that long (and that it's not even cheese!), I was convinced the *stuff* has no good nutritional value. Yes, it tastes good, and it had always been a comfort food. But it does nothing good for my health. It had to go.

And it's the same thing with money. It's *emotional* when I tell someone they need to cool out on spending money on unnecessary things like hair and nails while paying off debt. It's *emotional* when someone calls into *The Ramsey Show* and is struggling to deal with a family member who doesn't understand financial boundaries, and I have to walk them through how to say no to someone they love. It's *emotional* to tell someone that their mortgage payment on their dream house is suffocating them and if they don't sell it, they risk not being able to set their kids up for college and retire with dignity. Heck, it's even emotional to tell someone they need to stop eating out so much if they want to stop living paycheck-to-paycheck.

We all have our own financial Velveeta.

These habits are comforts in our lives. And for most of us, these comforts have been around for a long time. But just because some things are comforts, doesn't make them good.

Letting them go is an emotional process. But when you can understand the *why* behind the *what*, the *what* becomes a lot easier to accept. When it became clear why I needed to get Velveeta out of my life (it's truly terrible for me), it was way easier to let it go. The truth is, bad things can comfort us—but hey, good things can comfort us too.

Dr. Mark Hyman, a functional medicine physician and author, shared something around this topic that stuck with me: "We make the hard choices the healthy choices, and the easy choices the unhealthy choices. But when you flip that, you thrive."[17]

Hot take: We get to choose what we make hard, and we get to choose what we make easy. It's so easy to make something harder than it needs to be by kicking and flailing and being stubborn. And we can choose to make something that we considered hard a lot easier by learning about the benefits, being open to change, and setting up our habits to win.

When the doctor says to change your diet and get more exercise—or when the personal finance expert says to get on a budget and pay off your debt—on the outside we say, "Yeah, you're right, Doc." So we reluctantly follow the doctor's instructions for a while, but our heart isn't in it. It's still a suggestion we're following. We haven't owned it as our own mission and chosen way of life. The truth is, we don't really feel seen, and our feelings are hurt! Emotionally, we begin to grieve all we believe we're missing out on—we don't know any differently. And most days, we're looking for an excuse to fall off a wagon we never wanted to be on in the first place!

I felt the same way. When Sam and I were on our debt-free journey, there were days I felt I was missing out. Times I felt I deserved to be able to just buy a new car like everyone else. *Why couldn't I just be like everyone else?*

I was still in the "Yes, Doc" phase—or what Chris Voss describes as the "Yes, you're right" phase—of the mental negotiation. Voss is a former FBI hostage negotiator and author of the book *Never Split the Difference.* One of the takeaways from that book, which is so insightful, is the difference between the phrases "Yes, *you're* right" and "Yes, *that's* right."[18]

When we hear something like the Baby Steps or a new healthy diet, we know logic when we hear it. But we also may not fully agree or want to venture much farther down this road. So we say, "Yeah, you're right." Essentially, we hope we're saying enough to get the person off our back. It's like clocking into a job you hate—you have no real emotional buy-in, so you go through the motions, do the least to get by, and eventually quit.

However, the response that indicates true buy-in and ownership is "Yes, *that's* right." The barrier between "You're right" and "That's right" is personal buy-in. When the response is "Yes, that's right," you have accepted something as not just *a* truth but *the* truth, and therefore *your* truth. It's the difference between logical agreement and commitment.

When you get there, that's when forward movement can really take place. But here again, getting to this place is an emotional journey. Look, we're emotional beings. We were created to have feelings. But at the same time, our emotions don't have dominance over us. We are able to control and shift our emotional state.

One of my earliest introductions to this concept was a verse I grew up hearing from 2 Timothy that basically says, God didn't give us a spirit of fear—He gave us a spirit of power, love, and self-control. This verse is dealing with our emotions. It's telling us the truth of how we sometimes feel. But it's also reminding us that we have the power of self-control to shift our emotions or, better yet, control our actions amid them. And in my life, I've found that my emotions run rampant in the absence of information and facts. So this is a great scripture to lean on. It's telling us a fact: We have self-control.

My friend, mental-health expert Dr. John Delony, says it all the time: Facts are your friends. And learning the facts is the first step to uncovering and accepting the truth. When we know the facts, it's easier to curb and counter those emotional responses that aren't helpful. Remember this, because it will be a helpful tool to rely on during this process.

The facts and the truth are also in the labs. Earlier, I gave a general overview of what most people are going through with their money. Think of that as America's Lab Results. But here in a minute, we're going to look at *you* specifically. We're going to look at the results of your personal Financial Physical.

But you already know the prescribed plan of action. Spoiler alert: It's the Baby Steps. In chapter 2, we talked about all the different emotions folks experience when they walk through the Baby Steps. Some are great and can be motivating, but some are problematic and can cause folks to lose motivation, stop, or never start to begin with. Chances are, you fall into one of those camps.

And just like the example I gave earlier with the Golden Arches, your brain is going to immediately want to cling to what it knows. And if not immediately, trust me, it will happen at some point. Even for the most gung-ho Baby Steppers, our emotions eventually attempt to forsake us. It's just part of the journey.

But I want to encourage you to exercise that self-control and push through those emotions. And in this book, I'll show you exactly how.

I've had the opportunity to survey tens of thousands of people walking this road as part of my coaching webinars at Ramsey Solutions. In those sessions, we've asked folks to identify the emotions they are feeling and battling around starting and sticking to a plan with their money. And their responses jive with the same emotions Sam and I experienced ourselves:

1. Frustration
2. Fear
3. Guilt/Shame
4. Anger
5. Self-Pity

In many ways, these are similar to other step-by-step emotional processes that apply to different areas of life, like the five stages of grief or even the twelve-step Alcoholics Anonymous program. Now I'm no doctor (in any sense of the word), but I don't know if you can really go through a money journey like the Baby Steps without working through these emotions at some point along the way. Hey, you read my story! And the truth is, I spent way too much time wallowing in some of these phases. But hopefully, by shining a light on this emotional process, I can help you move through it more easily. It's not about making these emotions go away. It's about acceptance—moving forward in spite of the emotions and not letting them cause you to give up. It's about embracing power and self-control amid other, very real feelings.

That being said, it's time for *you* to embrace your proverbial paper gown, because this next part is going to be very uncomfortable and very revealing. To give your financial situation a proper once-over, we have to put it all out on the table. This is your chance to lay out all the goods. Monthly payments, debt balances, income—all of it. If you aren't ready to see it on paper, put this book down! You can pick it up later, preferably before the heart attack. (I don't want you to wait for a catastrophic event to change!)

But if you *are* ready now, I'm so proud of you. You're already making the journey from "You're right" to "*That's* right."

I want you to pause reading and take some time to fill in your Financial Physical. Now for your comfort, I've broken this into two parts: the initial checkup below and the full workup (you'll get access to that later). Full disclaimer: Writing it down will be hard. Choosing to show up and do something about it will feel harder. But remember what I said before about using facts to curb emotional responses. The big fact is this: You're not a victim. You get to choose what happens next. You get to choose which things you make harder and which things you make easier.

You're very much in control now. Hero status awaits.

YOUR FINANCIAL PHYSICAL: THE INITIAL CHECKUP

Think of this exercise as your first appointment. It won't take long—but take a deep breath, because this might sting a bit.

Cash Flow

Monthly Income

List every source of income you receive each month. Put the net amount—which is your paycheck *after* taxes are taken out.

Income Source	Monthly Amount ($)
Primary Job	
Side Hustle/Freelance	
Other	
Total Monthly Income	

Monthly Bills and Expenses

A big part of managing our money is knowing exactly what we spend it on. When we get clear on those numbers, we can start to identify our spending habits and trouble spots.

Expenses are usually grouped into two categories: fixed and variable. Fixed expenses are the amounts that stay the same each month, like rent or your car payment. Variable expenses are the ones that tend to fluctuate, like food, gas, or even your credit card payment. I listed a few categories below to help you get started, but list as many of these expenses as you can think of. Checking your last bank statement can give you a great starting point. And hey—no shame here! The goal is to get a clear, accurate picture of how you're really spending your money.

Expense	Monthly Amount ($)
Rent/Mortgage	
Utilities	
Phone and Internet	
Insurance	
Gas and Car Maintenance	
Groceries and Restaurants	
Subscriptions	
Car Payment	
Credit Card	
Student Loan	
Other	
Total Monthly Expenses	

Okay, now let's do some quick math. Take your total monthly income and subtract your total monthly expenses. This equation will give you your total margin—or as I like to call it, your "breathing room."

Monthly Income: $_______ - Monthly Expenses: $_______ = Breathing Room: $_______

Big Picture

Debts by Full Balance

It's time to look at the *total* balances on your debts. All of them. Because when we're only focused on what we can "afford" month to month, it's easy to forget the bigger elephant in the room—the real source of our stress and frustration.

Take your time and write out the full balance of every single debt you owe (everything but the mortgage). Whether it's a $30,000 student loan you owe to the federal government or a $300 spot you owe to a family member, now's the time to air it all out. (Don't estimate here. Log in to your accounts or look at your statements and get exact.)

Debt Type	Total Balance ($)
Credit Card #1	
Credit Card #2	
Student Loan	
Car Loan	
Personal Loan	
Installment Plans (Buy Now, Pay Later)	
Grandma	
IRS Debt	
Other	
Total Debt	

Annual Income

Now I want you to write out your total annual income. It's good to see, printed on the page, your total debt listed next to your total income. This is reality. So prepare yourself. It may be shocking. But it may also shine some light on why things feel the way they feel.

You'll also notice I'm asking for gross (before tax) and net (after tax) income separately. A lot of times we think, *Woo-hoo! I make $100,000 a year!* and instantly, our brain creates this image of a lifestyle we should be living. We tend to forget what our income looks like *after* Uncle Sam takes his pound of flesh.

Annual Gross Income	
Annual Net Income	

Total Debt: $_______ vs. Annual Net Income: $_______

Financial Reflection

Check In

It's time to be real with your emotions. Take a moment to think about how you're feeling now that you've seen your checkup results.

How would you feel if you didn't get paid next month?

Anxious | Neutral | Confident | Other: _______________

How would it affect your finances? (Remember, no relying on credit to cover the gaps. Be honest with yourself.)

____

____

____

How did you feel seeing your total debt listed next to your total income?

Shocked | Frustrated | Oh, crap! | Not as bad as I thought | Other: ______________

What were you surprised to see or learn as you completed this part of the physical?

____

____

____

What was your biggest takeaway?

____

____

____

I know, that wasn't easy. But I'm proud of you! Now, let's go make some progress.

Note: If you're feeling especially bold and want to complete the second part of your Financial Physical—the full workup—you can do that today. (More power to you!) You can find it on our resources page at jadewarshaw.com/resources. But if you're thinking, I've had enough for one day, *keep reading. You can go complete the full workup later.*

Brand-New Day

When Sam and I first started the Baby Steps, it was the Great Recession. As I was listening to *The Dave Ramsey Show* one day, I heard Dave say that, for him, the recession wasn't a disaster because he could buy real estate cheap. He talked about how he'd positioned himself to "fly above the storm" despite a national hardship. When Sam and I heard him say that, we locked in. Honestly, we were jealous. But not in a shade sort of way. In a motivating way. We wanted that *so bad* because we were in the center of the chaos. It was then and there that Sam and I made up our mind that the next time hard times hit, we'd be ready. We'd be better. We'd "fly above the storm." And we did.

Twelve years later, when the worst happened in the form of a global pandemic, Sam and I were able to batten down the hatches and ride out the storm because we'd worked the plan. In the end, nothing was lost. As a matter of fact, we benefited from the storm because real estate values continued to rise. We were "flying above the storm."

The takeaway lesson is this: Time is going to pass anyway. Five years, ten years, twenty years will tick by. Before you know it, you'll look up and be in one of three places: the same, worse off, or better.

In fifteen years, you could still be the same. Still playing the shell game. Still robbing Peter to pay Paul. You've consolidated all your debt into your home more than once. You still think leasing that car isn't a problem. But at the same time, you're still wondering why you can't seem to get ahead.

Or it could be worse. You could've experienced a job loss, and all that debt could come back to bite you in the butt. It could've taken you longer to find a new job than you expected. And since you had so much debt, you ate through your savings faster than you expected on those stupid monthly payments. Your *only choice* was relying on credit cards to stay afloat, which created an even bigger disaster. And all of that could cause you to consider filing chapter 7 bankruptcy, just like I hear on *The Ramsey Show* all the time.

But what if you make better choices? Because of the choices you make today, in fifteen years your financial life will be way better—as a matter of fact, fantastic. You haven't felt the weight of consumer debt in twelve years, it's so far in your rearview. And over the past twelve years, you've invested 15 percent of your income, and the last time you checked your retirement savings, it was almost to $300,000. *Let's go!* Not to mention, you've been intentional about throwing extra on your mortgage, so your home will be paid off at the end of this year. (And you don't want to brag—but when you checked Zillow, it was worth $700,000.) You're officially a net-worth millionaire! How you handle money has changed so much that it's hard to recognize who you used to be with money. What a blessing, this rich and satisfying life.

Listen, I'm not being dramatic with these examples on any front. This is not play play. Shoot, when the COVID-19 pandemic happened in 2020, I told my husband, "Wow, if we hadn't started the Baby Steps when we did back in '08, the pandemic would've taken us out. We'd either be homeless or living with my mom and dad." Now I know, that situation is kind of a once-in-a-century deal. But make no mistake—no one escapes unforeseen hardships. The time will pass, and the results of your actions will show. Full stop.

So, what will you choose? Because you just lost all plausible deniability, my friend. Whatever happens next, you have to own it fully as your choice—a choice you made in full knowledge of the probable outcome. For better or worse.

You can decide: *Forget Jade and her stupid book*, throw on Netflix, put the earbuds back in, and go back to living your life as you knew it. Or today can mark the dawning of a brand-new day. Shoot, a brand-new era. Let's call it your "Hero Era." It has a nice ring to it.

Which one will it be? Your choice.

CHAPTER FIVE

FRUSTRATION

Stop in the Name of Love

I woke up that morning to missed calls and voicemails from 1-800-PAY-ME, which is how I "lovingly" referred to debt collectors. But make no mistake, I hated when they called my phone. It felt like an invasion of privacy—like all my mistakes were taunting me with each buzz.

I never answered. I'd tried that before. I'd tried indulging them, but it never worked. By now, I'd given up on that. I'd learned from experience that I didn't have what they wanted. They wanted money *now*—yesterday, really—and Sam and I didn't have it. They'd want to set up a payment plan, but I'd only be lying if I accepted it. Because we were focused on other, more pressing debts, they wouldn't be getting a payment from me for a very long time. So instead, I just learned to live with their constant buzzing in my ear. It was something I accepted.

I swiped the screen to clear the notifications from my phone and tried to act as if it were nothing more than swatting a gnat away from my face. Then I tried to move on with the day. But the calls kept coming. More and more persistent.

Buzz.

Every hour.

Buzz.

Several times per hour.

Buzz. Buzz.

Because we had multiple cards, with multiple banks, and many were in my name alone.

Buzz. Buzz. Buzz.

I kept going about my day.

That afternoon, Sam and I were out running errands, driving down the road in our old Jeep Liberty (our only car because we'd sold off the Hummer). We were heading to the bank to make a deposit. Since we both taught music lessons as a side hustle—sixty bucks an hour—we made this trip frequently. And on this particular day, we needed to get the cash into the account ASAP so we could pay our rent on time.

As we drove toward that bank, like clockwork: *Buzz.* Freaking 1-800-PAY-ME, again and again. With each ring I found myself feeling more and more frantic on the inside. Each time I'd silence the phone, I'd also stuff down whatever I was feeling. Suddenly, however, there was no room left to stuff my emotions.

Buzz.

I was being swarmed, and I couldn't ignore it anymore! I couldn't breathe. I couldn't exhale. There was no room left, no oxygen left. I couldn't take it anymore. I'd had it!

"Stop!" I finally burst out. "Pull the car over!!"

"Wait, what?" a completely bewildered Sam asked.

"I've had it!" I shrieked. "I can't take it anymore! Pull the car over, *now!*"

"Okay," Sam said calmly, sensing that I'd hit a point of no return.

We'd almost made it to the bank—we were in a gravel lot off the back alley behind it. Sam parked in a remote spot and kept the Jeep running. It was summertime in south Florida, and it was *hot*. Keeping the air conditioner on was a necessity. But the moment we parked, as if on cue, the A/C immediately began to struggle to keep the car cool. The vent blew blasts of lukewarm air onto our faces, and it only seemed to fuel my flames.

This stupid Jeep! I thought. (I'll save you the more colorful language running through my mind at that moment.) I was deep into my feelings. And I finally began spewing it all out.

"All this sacrifice! And for what?" I sobbed. "We have *one car*, and the A/C is busted. Chase is blowing me up! We have roommates, and we're *still* barely making rent. We're busting our butts, and we're *still* overdrawing every month. We've toiled and toiled, but we've barely gotten anywhere!"

With each passing moment, I was getting more frantic and more desperate. I was at the end of my rope.

"Let's just take this money and . . . and pay on the credit card so they'll leave me alone!" I said, grabbing the cash we planned to deposit and shaking it. "I just want them to leave me alone!"

All we needed was $230 to get somebody, anybody, off my back. I knew it was rent money, but I didn't care. I also knew the $230 would only satisfy *one* of the many collectors calling me. This wasn't a real solution—but I didn't care. I wasn't thinking straight. I'll never forget how pivotal and out of reach that $230 seemed.

In that moment, there was nothing I wouldn't do to get that money, but it also felt like there was *nothing left* to do to get that money. Sam and I were sacrificing so much. What was wrong? Why was this happening?

What's Going On?

Frustration: *The rising sense of annoyance you feel when you believe your results don't match your efforts.*

Frustration is like being confined by a straitjacket. You can try squirming, wrenching, and struggling to bust out, but in a matter of minutes, your muscles are tired, your mind is tired, and your patience to continue the struggle is going out the window with each tug.

It's the irritation we've all felt of trying to get a stubborn zipper free from the cloth that's blocking it or attempting to untie an angry knot of extension cords. The thread you pull in the sewing kit, thinking it will loosen the knot, only makes the mess more tangled. *Ugh!*

The whole process is enough to raise your temperature, raise your temper, *and* tap dance on your last good nerve. It's enough to make you want to throw up your hands and say, "That's it! I just can't do it. I tried. It didn't work—I give up."

The urge to allow frustration to persist without leaning into a new or better solution is pretty normal. You get so zoomed into your situation, it's like that old adage: You can't see the forest for the trees. And so we let our frustration drift into complacency.

"Nothing I do seems to work."

"I'm doing everything I can."

"It just is what it is."

The jacket with the messed-up zipper is still in the closet; you just resolved to wear it open and be cold. That tangled bunch of extension cords remains in the attic, waiting to annoy you again the next time you need them. The tangled thread mocks you from the sewing kit. And the straitjacket in your life that once had you struggling to break free has now weirdly become part of your daily life. You've just learned to ignore it or work around it, even though the truth is, you still can't really breathe.

When it comes to getting on track with your money, the story doesn't change. The struggle is real. The frustration is real. And if we aren't careful, it can result in a sense of complacency that is very real. I remember feeling like I was in financial quicksand at times. No matter how Sam and I struggled to get out, we just kept sinking. I remember feeling frustrated with slow progress, lack of progress, and sometimes flat-out going backward.

It was enough to make me want to throw my hands up and say, "That's it! I just can't do it." And it's exactly what happened for me in the stupid Jeep that day. That's what was driving me to consider doing something rash.

Thankfully, in that moment, my husband knew me well enough not to make any sudden movements that would escalate the situation. He's always been the yin to my yang—the balance I need so badly. He remained his emotionally even self, and for about an hour after my outburst, we sat in that hot car together. Crying, venting, lamenting, and finally, strategizing a new plan to move forward. One that *didn't* involve using our rent money to satisfy an abusive debt collector.

After the storm clouds of tears and emotions parted, our frustrations gave way to an *Aha!* moment. And suddenly, we began to see beyond the trees in our own forest.

Maybe we were going about this all wrong!

The Way You Do the Things You Do

Fact: We were well into our debt-free journey, and we'd done a lot of things right.
Fact: We had made a lot of intentional sacrifices.
Fact: We had made a decent amount of progress paying/selling off almost $163,000 of debt.
Fact: We were still doing some things "our way" money-wise.

That last fact was the problem. This right here is what leads so many of us down the path of frustration to the point of wanting to quit. You feel like you're doing the most, *and it's still not working.* But if you step back and are truly honest with yourself, you may learn that you're doing a few things incorrectly—intentionally or unintentionally. The devil is in the details. Now, those details can torment you, like they did me, and make you want to give up. Or focusing in on the details can drive you to your destination faster.

Ultimately, if you want to be effective and if you want to reduce frustration, the way you do the things you do matters! The way you work this plan matters.

I'll be honest. I'm not sure you can remove the frustration completely because this whole journey is a learning process. Frustration is part of learning and embracing new things. But there are levels, and the key to letting frustration drive you forward instead of stopping you dead in your tracks is asking the right questions.

That day in the car, I remember thinking, *Why is this so hard? Is there something we're not doing right?* Those questions led us to essentially do an audit of our biggest frustrations. That day in the car, Sam and I sat and went over the details of what we were doing with our money with a fine-tooth comb. Here's what it looked like:

Frustration Audit

Step 1: Identify our main areas of frustration.

The first thing we had to do was clearly determine our major sources of frustration. For me, it was threefold:

1. Debt collectors
    - I needed them to go away.
    - They were ruining my peace.

  - I was starting to feel some type of way because they were calling mostly me, not Sam. That's not good, because it was creating resentment toward my own spouse, my *teammate*! We were in this together, and allowing these calls to drive a wedge between Sam and me needed to stop.
2. Overdraft fees
  - I was sick of it. If logging into our bank account and seeing a sea of red wasn't enough, then I had to swallow my pride and get on the phone and plead with a customer service agent, who I was at the mercy of, to remove some of the charges.
  - We overdrew several times a month, and I couldn't figure out why.
  - It was eating away at our progress and making me want to quit budgeting altogether.
3. Nothing extra
  - Sam and I were always at zero in our bank account. So if something came up, we were screwed.
  - We had a constant sense of "living on the edge."
  - We found ourselves arguing about whose fault it was.

Step 2: Find where those frustrations link to the plan.

Next, we looked at where each of our areas of frustration correlated to certain points of the plan, which was fairly simple:

Debt pay-off issues = Baby Step 2 and Debt Snowball principles
Overdrafts and cash flow issues = Budgeting
No extra money = Baby Step 1

Step 3: Compare our actual behavior to the plan.

Now that we knew where to look, the two of us began to audit our *behavior* as it relates to the plan. We compared what we were doing to what the plan actually says to do. And this is where our *I've had it!* moment turned into an *Aha!* moment for each of our areas of frustration.

Frustration Area: Debt pay-off issues

How we were paying off debt:
Paying minimums on our important bills and putting all extra toward the smallest debt.

How the plan says to pay off debt:
Pay the minimums on *all debts* to keep them current. And put all extra toward the smallest debt.

Aha:
Somewhere along the line, we had decided that credit cards weren't as important as the car payment. So we stopped making minimum payments on those, thinking

we could free up money faster to pay the car off if we put off the credit cards. Clearly, that backfired in a major way. From now on, minimums had to be paid. So we decided to hit Pause on our pay-off to get everything current and then push Play on paying minimums—and then put everything else toward the smallest debt.

Frustration Area: Overdrafts and cash flow issues

How we were budgeting:
We were giving every single dollar an assignment and spending until we reached zero dollars in the bank account.

How the plan says to budget:
Give every single dollar an assignment, but you should never have zero dollars in your account. You should always have a cushion line item so that you aren't overdrawing if something unexpected comes out of your account during the month.

Aha:
Truthfully, I had never noticed this teaching before. What a watershed moment it was for us to realize it's a good thing to have a bit of money padding your account! This was a small behavior Sam and I had overlooked unintentionally. And now that we were digging in, it turned out to be an easy fix.

Frustration Area: No extra money

How we were approaching saving:
We had no money saved and had started Baby Step 2 anyway.

How the plan says to approach saving:
You need $1,000 saved in Baby Step 1 before you start Baby Step 2.

Aha:
To be honest, this one wasn't really an *Aha!*—my hard-headed self just needed to be set straight. And I ended up learning the lesson the hard way. I thought we didn't need it. We were so desperate to get out of debt and so used to not having any savings that we kept putting it off. I just saw it as us putting more money toward paying off debt. I was wrong! Sam and I needed that starter emergency fund so that the small things didn't throw off our progress.

The mistakes we made were small but had a huge impact. It was like leaving the car in Park but slamming on the gas. You don't get anywhere. You just burn costly fuel. Now we can all look at *that* situation and say, "Well, *duh*! You've gotta put the car in drive if you want it to go."

The same thing applies here. The way you do the things you do matters. So instead of quitting because of your frustration, I want you to do an audit. Go over the situation with a fine-tooth comb, just like we did. By doing this, you'll find the problem . . . and the solution right there in the Baby Steps.

Okay, it's time to get tactical. Right now, no matter where you are in the Baby Steps, take a moment and do your own frustration audit. Use the worksheet provided to write out your top three areas of frustration, link those frustrations to the Baby Step or plan teaching that goes with it, and audit your behavior compared with what the plan says. This will lead you to your *Aha!* moments, giving you clarity on how to solve those root issues.

Go do that now—I'll wait.

FRUSTRATION AUDIT

Step 1: Identify your top three areas of frustration.

Write them down and add some notes about why they're so frustrating.

1. ____

____

____

2. ____

____

____

3. ____

____

____

Step 2: Find where those frustrations link to the plan.

Look at your areas of frustration compared to the Baby Steps teachings. Where do you see connection points or overlap?

____

____

____

____

Step 3: Compare your actual behavior to the plan.

Now audit your *behavior* as it relates to the plan. Look at what you're doing versus what the plan actually says to do.

Frustration Area 1: ______________________

How we're doing this:

____

____

How the plan says to do this:

____

____

Aha:

____

____

Frustration Area 2: ______________________

How we're doing this:

____

____

How the plan says to do this:

____

____

Aha:

____

____

Frustration Area 3: ____________________

How we're doing this:

____

____

How the plan says to do this:

____

____

Aha:

____

____

Don't let those *Aha!* moments go to waste! To gain some momentum, go make the adjustments you need to make.

If you are experiencing a lot of frustration, you'll likely find discrepancies between your behavior and what the plan says. As you get aligned with the plan, you'll find that some fixes will be quick and relatively painless, like adding a cushion line item to your budget or backing down your investing to 15 percent. Others might take a little longer to set straight, like Sam and I getting current and *then* paying the minimums on our credit cards.

The point is, what you do with this discovery is pivotal. It's a decision you are making. You get to determine how long you stay trapped in this emotional state of financial frustration. Will you say, "I've had it—I quit!" or "I've had it—*Aha!* Let's get it right"?

I say, let's get it right! Because no one likes the frustration of being stuck in financial quicksand. So instead of letting frustration swallow you whole and leave you in a pit of complacency, let's swallow our pride, get out of this mess right way, and move on.

You've Really Got a Hold on Me

"But Jade, here's the thing . . ." **inserts excuse here**

We know what the problem is. We learn what the solution to the problem is . . . and we *still* try to find an excuse not to do it! Talking to folks on *The Ramsey Show*, I hear this pattern often, and I've even done it many times in my own life. When this happens, you can boil it down to a comfort zone issue. The pain and frustration of what you're experiencing now hasn't yet exceeded the pain of changing. Think about that for a minute.

For example, at one point in our journey (further in than I'd like to admit), Sam and I still had a credit card. It was a dinky $500-limit credit card, but I insisted that we keep it. It was a security blanket of sorts for me. Since we traveled so much for work and were on the road with hotels and transportation and all the unexpected costs, having it just made me feel better. The only problem was, we kept running it up and paying it off, running it up and paying it off. Wasn't the point to pay off the debt and be done with it? I was starting to feel like a dog chasing its tail because, each month, instead of putting a hard-earned $500 onto something meaningful like paying off our car, I had to pay off that dadgum credit card. Again. For the hundredth time.

The truth was, knowing we had that credit card as a crutch somehow made us say yes to things we probably would have said no to if we were only using the cash we had in the bank. The solution to my frustration was lying right there in guidance from the Baby Steps. I just had to embrace it emotionally.

1. Cut up the credit card. *You can't solve a problem while simultaneously creating it.*
2. Budget for everything you might spend money on for the month. (This requires foresight and intentionality.)
3. Create a new budget each month because each month is different.

The truth was, by then we'd done the job long enough to know what we needed to budget for. We were just too lazy and too hardheaded and comfortable to do it. We'd looked to the solution that was easiest and most comfortable *on the surface*—not the solutions that would serve us best and actually get us where we wanted to be long term. So Sam and I were out there busting our butts to pull ourselves out of debt but not making real progress because we kept adding to the pile. And that's what frustration is: toil without traction.

We'd fallen into the dysfunction of being comfortable with our frustrations, comfortable with our complacent behavior. Like Dave Ramsey would say, we were like babies sitting in a dirty diaper—*I may be sitting in a mess, but it's warm and it's mine. Don't take it from me.*

But I'd finally gotten to the point where the pain and frustration of paying off that card each month was greater than the pain of change and embracing the solution. It was time for me to cut up the card. And when I did, it was like being let loose from the straitjacket that had been holding us back from moving the way we needed to.

It comes down to this: Your frustration can be an amazing catalyst for change. It helps you feel that the pain of staying the same is greater than the pain of change. So instead of letting your frustration cause you to quit, let it drive you to evaluate, audit, and realign your behavior.

Think

If you still feel the emotions of your old excuses keeping you frustrated and stuck, think of what your toil-without-traction is costing you.

Your frustration is stealing your power. The longer you stay frustrated, the more you drain your power. And not to get corny on you, but in this case, I'm using POWER as an acronym that represents a lot of important things: your Peace, your Options, your Why, your Efficiency, and your Results.

Peace

First off, when you let nagging frustrations persist, they become these annoying nuisances that slowly but surely eat away at your peace. Death by a thousand cuts.

My example was 1-800-PAY-ME. Anyone remember the show *American Gladiators* from the '80s? They used to have this one-on-one match called the Joust, where a gladiator and a competitor each stood on a small, raised platform with a big club that looked like a giant Q-tip. The point of the game was to use the giant Q-tip to knock the other person off the platform and into the pit.

This was my game with 1-800-PAY-ME. Only I didn't have a Q-tip of my own. Each call was a blow attempting to knock me, inch by inch, off my platform of peace until, finally, I found myself falling.

Maybe your game looks different. You've grown complacent with the frustration of paycheck-to-paycheck living, but each hit of the Q-tip has you losing more and more of what little peace you do have. If your daughter gets sick and you have to stay home, missing out on that pay—blow. The phone bill is $15 more this month, *ugh*—another blow. That check is gonna end up getting here on Monday instead of Friday—blow. Your mother-in-law makes a side comment about your financial situation again—blow (below the belt). Your child talking excitedly about the college he or she wants to attend that you know you can't afford—blow.

Each hit is just stealing more of your peace.

During those moments in my life, both financial and otherwise, where I've felt myself falling off my platform of peace, I remember Proverbs 4:23: "Guard your heart above all else, for it determines the course of your life" (NLT). "Guard" is just another word for "protect." And peace has to do with the state of your heart. When the heart is not at peace—ooh baby.

I needed to get this money thing right to protect my peace, and so do you! And that means, get the heck out of Dodge! Let's move quickly and with intensity. If you're faced with frustration, make the necessary changes. If you don't, you and your finances remain exposed—and that makes it tough to block those hits. When you're living life knowing that you are one push of the Q-tip away from everything crashing down, that's not financial peace.

Options

Let's talk about options for a minute. Remember when I said that sometimes we get so bogged down in the frustration of our own situation that we can't see the forest for the trees? We're so busy hacking through the forest of frustration, we have had no time to think about what's *beyond* our frustrations.

It makes me remember one day when I was out to lunch with a lifelong friend of mine, Jasmine, and her mother, Laura. While sitting at the restaurant, we were talking—dreaming, really—about options and possibilities for the new year.

"If you could do anything career-wise, what would it be?" I asked Laura. She cocked her head to the side, searching for an answer. After several beats, she finally replied, "I have no idea."

In a nutshell, she began to explain how the frustrations of her money and relationships had kept her focused on just keeping her head above water. In other words, she didn't have time to think about *options.* And that's so true, isn't it? When you're frustrated just making monthly payments to satisfy all your bills, all you think about is getting the job that brings in enough to pay your bills—not the job you'd really love to do someday. When you're frustrated with a vehicle you owe $32,000 on and you're upside-down, it's hard to imagine the option of saving up to pay cash for a car.

Don't let frustration steal your options. No matter where you are, take the time to intentionally think about all your life can be. Imagine positive things like, *One day, I can be debt-free. One day, I can have a career I love. One day, I can pay cash to finish my degree. One day, I can have peace with my money.* For me, thinking of this passage of Scripture helps get my mind right: "Finally, brothers and sisters, whatever is true, whatever is noble, whatever is right, whatever is pure, whatever is lovely, whatever is admirable—if anything is excellent or praiseworthy—think about such things" (Philippians 4:8 NIV). It gives us the permission and space to dream and paint a beautiful picture of what we'd like our lives to look like.

Why

You've probably heard that your *why* for doing something is important. It's the reason you set out on a money journey to begin with. When you succumb to frustrations, it's easy to forget what it's all for.

One day during our debt-free journey, I was on a jog, and I had what I'd call a true vision. In my mind's eye, I saw myself walking a child down the sidewalk to school. In the vision, I perceived that I was debt-free, our home was just up the street, and I had the financial freedom and autonomy to be there for my son to walk him to and from school each day. I hadn't realized that I'd completely stopped jogging and was staring into the future until the picture faded from my mind and I snapped back to reality.

From that moment on, I held that vision in my heart. I felt like God gave me that clear why to keep me going. But the frustration I felt with the math and timeline of our debt pay-off threatened to choke out that vision.

At one point, Sam and I had been working so hard to get our show off the ground. We knew that if we could get booked two weeks a month, consistently, we were golden. But instead, we kept getting booked for one-off performances. It was good, but far from getting the job done. And then it happened: Princess Cruises booked us for six months straight. It was like all our dreams had come true. We immediately calculated the amount of debt we'd be able to pay off and were jumping up and down with excitement.

But then the worst happened. The day after our first performance on Princess, we got an email saying that we weren't the right fit for their audience, and they were pulling out on all our dates. Our hearts sank. I was so frustrated that I wondered if we should just give it up. I remember us flying home from that trip with the wind completely out of our sails.

But that vision, that why, was like a fire. I knew what God had told me. Instead of giving up, Sam and I went home and got back to work. It was in that season that I learned the true meaning of a mantra I have to this day: "The stronger the why, the stronger the try." When you find your why—your purpose, your vision, the goal for your money—don't let anything hinder you from getting to it.

When Princess dropped our dates, I was so frustrated. There were moments when I questioned everything we were working for. But I had to block out all those doubts. Suddenly, Galatians 5:7 applied directly to me: "You were running [the race] well; who has interfered and prevented you from obeying the truth?" (AMP). We couldn't let that setback stop us. And I'll pass that encouragement on to you: When you find your why, treat it as the truth—and continue to go after it. Don't let frustrations stop you from running your race.

Efficiency

Just practically speaking, when you let yourself stay in a frustrated state, you are stealing efficiency—and in the money journey, this usually equates to valuable time and effort.

Remember my friend's mom, Laura, the one I mentioned before? Well, for years I'd shared with her the power of the Debt Snowball and the Baby Steps—the ideas that focusing on one task at a time allows you to get to your goals faster and more efficiently. And no shade, but it must be said: To this day, Laura is *still* frustrated and in debt, doing the absolute most. Meanwhile, Sam and I got a much later start and have been debt-free for years. And we started with more debt and less income.

Frustration costs you efficiency. All toil, no traction. So ask yourself, in this story, do you want to be my friend's mom, or do you want to be Sam and me?

I'll help you out. Change is a choice, and today you can choose. Put your valuable time and effort to good use. Whether it's listing your debts from smallest to largest (the first step of the Debt Snowball method) or using that hunk of savings to knock out a few of your debts, choose efficiency over frustration *today*.

Results

My good friend Anita was interested in the Baby Steps for a long time, but her husband, James, wasn't fully onboard. He's a great guy—he just couldn't understand the "need to go to these extremes." Anita and James had a decent amount of debt, almost $100,000 total. For years, Anita was frustrated waiting around for James to get onboard, but finally she had her *I've had it!* moment and quickly turned it to an *Aha!*

Just because he's not fully onboard doesn't mean I can't do my best, she realized. *Slow progress is better than no progress.*

She implemented what I now call a Share, Do, Share routine. She shared the budget with James and what she planned to do with the margin, then she did it, then she shared with James that she did it. All the while, Anita continued to budget for the things that made her husband feel peace. Sure, this caused progress to be slower, but at least things were moving. And again, slow progress is better than no progress. In the end, Anita was able to pay off all $100,000 of debt. Could it have been faster? Sure. But she's not thinking about that now. She's just happy it's done!

Sometimes, when you're facing frustrating barriers, you have to adopt Anita's way of getting results. To quote Mariah Carey, "I did the best I can with what I got!" Period. There's always something you can do to create change in your situation. You don't have to let your results get sidelined by frustration.

Signed, Sealed, Delivered

The moral of the story is this: Some level of frustration on this journey is par for the course. But if it's got you stuck or ready to throw in the towel, there's a problem. Thankfully, for every financial frustration you face, there's a solution waiting in the right financial plan. And it's usually found in you getting out of your comfort zone. The longer you wait, the more there is at stake.

Don't sacrifice your POWER anymore. Do an audit and go from *I've had it* to *Aha!* to *get it right*. We're done with toil and no traction. This time we're moving past the frustration—not letting it hold us back.

CHAPTER SIX

FEAR

Waiting on the World to Change

I'll never forget March 13, 2020, for three reasons:

1. It was the day of my baby shower for my second child.
2. It was Friday the 13th—a forever signal of bad luck.
3. It was the day the world shut down to "stop the spread" of COVID-19.

We had officially entered a global pandemic, I was eight months pregnant with our daughter, and Sam's and my business in the cruise industry was closed until further government notice. What I needed was a good stiff drink, or three, but of course that wasn't possible because of the baby. When I think back about the amount of fear threatening to overtake me in that moment, *Whew, child!* It's hard to even put into words. I was in shock.

We had an emergency fund, but we were in the process of restocking it. Luckily, we still received money from contract work we did for our church. And luckily, we didn't have any debt aside from our mortgage. But now, our family would essentially be living on one-third of our previous income. I couldn't breathe—and this time, it wasn't because our daughter was pushing on my rib cage. It was because I felt *all* the fear!

When I considered what the future might hold, all I had were questions. *How long will this last? Will my baby be safe? Can we live on one-third of our income? Will we lose our home?* My fears had my mind racing at full tilt. I can honestly say that it was one of the scariest times I've experienced in my life. It was the type of fear that has the potential to paralyze a person.

But that couldn't happen! Sam and I had a toddler at home and a baby on the way. We had a talent agency full of people all over the globe that needed us to be cool, calm, and collected. And we had a bank account that needed us to have a level head, not react impulsively. If he and I were gonna get through this, our fears could not be controlling the wheel of that metaphorical car.

"Two weeks to stop the spread" ballooned into eighteen months to stop the spread for the cruise industry. And that's how long it took before our business resumed fully. Eighteen months.

That year and a half, I'll be honest, kinda felt like we were living within the plot of *The Pursuit of Happyness*—one of my favorite movies of all time, but not one I ever wanted to relate to at this level. If you're familiar, it's based on the true story of salesman Chris Gardner (played by Will Smith) and his journey from rock bottom to finding true success. But for most of that movie, Gardner was facing terrifying situation after terrifying situation!

In one scene, Gardner returns to his apartment after a long day, only to find that the locks on his door have been changed; he and his four-year-old son have been evicted, their few belongings strewn on the sidewalk as though they had no value. With no place to go for the night, Gardner uses a subway token to buy them some time to come up with a plan. They ride the train aimlessly for a while until he ultimately takes his son to the only place he can think of for them to sleep for the night: the bathroom in the subway terminal. As you'd expect, it's filthy, but it has a lock on the door.

You can physically feel the weight of his fear and desperation through the screen as hobos and drug addicts slam on the bathroom door throughout the night, trying to get in. Gardner holds his son tight and begins to cry. This is rock bottom. This is scary stuff. But instead of giving in, he treats the next morning as a brand-new day. He finds a shelter where they can stay temporarily. And over the course of the movie, he continues to stare his fears in the face, from signing up for a Wall Street internship with no prior experience, to engaging in meetings with wealthy clients while being homeless himself. He powers forward through his fears, working through them, in them, and, against all odds, eventually overcoming them.

COVID was our "Pursuit of Happyness season," so to speak. Sure, I wasn't locked in a subway bathroom sobbing. (I was locked in my own, far cleaner, bathroom sobbing.) But the persistent fear was there. And it was very real.

Back in chapter 4, I talked about being in a position to fly above a storm in this season. And while Sam and I did, it felt like the storm we were flying over was a Category-5 hurricane. Sure, we were above it, but if I looked down, all I saw was a dark, ominous sky prepared to utterly destroy us. At times, that's what I was afraid *would* happen.

It's easy to allow these fears to paralyze us and keep us from getting where we truly want to be with our money.

No matter how prepared we were for the storm, that season could have taken us down if we let those fears get the best of us and drive our actions. But like Chris Gardner, we realized that fighting through our biggest fears to get to where we wanted to be was worth it—if we didn't quit. So we didn't.

The challenges we faced during that season put us to the test. Fear has a way of doing that. But if you can make it through, in the end you can look back and see how much you grew and matured. And eventually you'll be able to see the purpose it served in your life.

Clarity

Fear is an interesting concept and a tricky emotion that, in my opinion, gets a bad rap sometimes. Is it good? Is it bad? Is it something to get over or work through? Can it—should it—be eliminated? Or is it healthy to keep fear around? All good questions. But before we can answer them, let's look at what fear is. If you were to look up a more formal definition, it defines *fear* as the sense of being in threat of danger, pain, or discomfort—real or imagined. But if I were to describe fear, especially the fears we face with our money, I'd word it a little differently. It'd sound more like this:

Fear: *A negative expectation of the future based on rational or irrational beliefs.*

I added the element about the future because, if you think about it, fear is rarely about what's happening in the moment. It's really about our perceived outcome or what we think is going to happen in the future. *If* I do this, *then* some negative thing will happen in the future.

And let me just offer a little validation and say that fear is . . . normal. Back in chapter 3, we talked about that annoying Check Engine light. When we're broke and that light flashes on, and we get that pit in our stomach or that flash of cold sweat, it's not about the moment; it's about what we believe will happen later. Just like that, our mind begins to paint a picture of future events:

> "Shoot! There's no way I'm getting out of that shop for under $1,000!"
>
> "If I don't get the money soon, I'm gonna end up broken down on the side of the road."
>
> "There goes our trip to New York next month."

Now go back and look at those definitions of fear. I want to remind you of the part of our definition that references those beliefs being *rational* or *irrational*—or, in the more formal case, threats that are *real* or *imagined*. When fear strikes and our mind begins painting a picture of the future, I'd argue that the picture is almost always based on our personal beliefs, what we've seen and heard most, and our own previous experiences. In many ways, fear is like Chat GPT—it doesn't spin up original content. It can only run on the information that's been fed into it.

Oh snap! You already know where I'm going with this!

When it comes to taking action with our money, it's the same way. We get scared of what we think will happen in the future. But that negative expectation is based on our own "Chat GPT," not necessarily what's true.

"But Jade, isn't fear also a safety mechanism that keeps us from doing something stupid or harmful? If I feel fear, maybe I ought to listen!"

Well played.

Figuring out whether our money fears are real and rational—or imagined and irrational—is something we must decipher if we want to make progress in the midst of overcoming our fears.

When it comes to this money journey, one way I can tell if my fear is well-founded or if I just need to get a grip is to look at the clarity of fear. Now I'm not saying this is a 100 percent, foolproof method. But in most cases, I find that my irrational fears tend to be ambiguous as they relate to the negative outcome I'm afraid of.

> "If I get on a budget, I'll probably screw the whole thing up."

> "I'm scared I'll miss out on all the things I want to do!"

> "I don't want to do it if it's gonna make our kids suffer."

> "It's gonna take forever, and I won't be able to enjoy my life."

All of these are fear-based statements, but the outcomes are vague. What do you mean "screw the whole thing up"? What does it mean for "our kids to suffer"? This is an indicator that you haven't truly given the matter any deep thought—you're just riding the whim of your initial feeling—whereas my more rational fears tend to have a more specific outcome. Those sound a bit more concrete:

> "If I take on a side hustle on Saturdays, I'm afraid it won't be worth it because of what I'll need to pay a sitter. And then the whole thing will be a waste of time and effort."

This is a much clearer, more specific thought. One that I can easily get the answer to and work through. The good news is that both rational and irrational fears are completely normal, and both can be dealt with.

Now that we know what fear is and how to discern whether a specific fear is rational or irrational, let's take our discovery a step further and break down some of the different types of fear.

Shouldn't Matter, But It Does

Fear is like the same person wearing different costumes—it can show up in a lot of different ways in our lives. There's no way I can cover every category here, but when it comes to changing money habits, these are the five main types of fear that Sam and

I experienced. And I've found the same to be true for a lot of the folks I've coached over the years. Being able to identify the fear type you struggle with can be the first step in working through it.

Fear of the Unknown

When I was a kid, about five, I shared a room with my older sister. In the light of day, that room was great. I could see the two twin beds. I could see my lovable stuffed animals perched on my bed. I could open the closet with no problem to find my sparse little wardrobe hung up all neatly. I could rummage through my large brown trunk full of dress-up clothes with no fear at all. I could even see the details of the popcorn-textured ceiling (an interior design staple of the 1980s).

My room was great—so why was it that, once night fell, it all changed? If, heaven forbid, my eyes popped open in the middle of the night, my little-kid imagination ran rampant. Suddenly, my sister's bed across the room was totally lost in the darkness, and I felt all alone. My beloved stuffed animals suddenly looked like scary shadows. And the closet . . . don't even get me started! There was a monster inside, I just knew it! And instead of wearing Grandma's fun dress-up clothes, that monster was dressed as the scariest thing my kindergarten brain could imagine. Picture Freddy Krueger's tattered clothes. (Again, very '80s.)

One night during these terrifying imaginings, I pulled my teddy bear tea party blanket over my head—then had a spark of genius. I jumped out of my bed and threw the lights on.

"Hey!" my sister huffed in an irritated tone, eyes squinting at the brightness.

The light revealed that she was right there, lying in her bed—still in the room after all! I looked around and found my stuffed animals back to their normal, playful selves. Then I headed straight to the closet and flung it wide open to prove to myself everything was as it should be there too. But to my shock, there *was* something there: a giant spider, chilling high in the right corner of the wall. A wolf spider, for sure.

Okay, it wasn't the scary monster I'd imagined, but this bad boy still needed to be dealt with! I was going to need help. I dragged my sister out of bed. She took one look and went to get my dad. Raid was sprayed, the eight-legged beast was no more, and my fears of what was in the closet—of what was hiding in the dark—died that night with the spider (mostly).

It's amazing what a little light can reveal. It can show us what's actually there, down to the details. It can show us the truth of the matter. And it can reveal things that need to be dealt with—sprayed with Raid and squashed, never to return.

We all have a story like this from our childhood. So why is it, then, that as adults we forget the importance of shedding light on the dark areas we face in our lives? Why do we still continue to keep our money monsters in the closet? I'll tell you why: because we've let fear of the unknown take over our emotions.

This is one of the big fears that comes up around dealing with your money. You don't even want to look at the reality of your finances and how you're spending because you're afraid of what you might find. It's the "monster in the closet" debacle all over again—we're afraid of what we don't know, and we let that fear keep us in the dark along with our money problems. And I find that this fear takes shape in two ways:

1. You don't truly know the state of your finances. And the idea of pulling back the curtain or looking under the rug makes your knees weak. Now, hopefully you dealt with this a few chapters ago when I encouraged you to commit and lay it all out. But if you didn't, it's likely because of this type of fear.
2. You are afraid of what working the Baby Steps will actually *feel* like. The truth is, maybe you've never committed to something that requires this level of sacrifice, so that feeling is new territory. Most of us have never done the things the Baby Steps are suggesting we do, and the way taking those steps will feel is a big, scary question mark. So instead of going forward with everything out in the light, you've decided to keep the lights off. You keep telling yourself that ignorance is bliss. But you and I both know, ignorance is not bliss—it's broke. And truthfully, keeping things in the dark is likely causing you more angst for the simple reason that you can't see what's there.

We've all heard that Bible verse that says when you find the truth, the truth will set you free. Light and truth go hand in hand. Wherever you shine a light, truth emerges—and that truth has the ability to set you free . . . if you choose. If you ask me, today is a good day to open the closet, turn the lights on, and get free.

Fear of the Known

Some of you are in a slightly different boat: You know what the situation is, the lights are on, and you realize you have a big, scary problem on your hands. You know what you have to do—open a can of whoop ass on your debts and finally make your money submit—but you're scared of the process. Your fear feels more like the intimidation of having to square up against a big, strong bully.

Someday you're going to fight, and you're going to win—but it ain't gonna be pretty. You're procrastinating and putting off the proverbial black eye and busted nose you may walk away with by stalling and biding time with minimum payments and excuses, hoping to avoid the big swings.

Fear of Change

Fear of change is next up on the list—and boy, is it a doozy! Have you ever felt yourself on the cusp of something *big*? I mean, you come across something that just rocks your world, man. It could be a sermon you hear at church, a motivational talk at a self-help rally, or a podcast that convinces you this diet is the one that will change *everything*. Emotions are high, the arguments are compelling, and the logic makes total sense! But the moment the clouds clear from your head, you start to count the cost of what it will actually take to put those world-rocking changes into action. Suddenly your elation and revelation turns to a dizzy, sick feeling in your stomach as you think of all your normal habits you have to exchange for, well, different habits. You realize there will be things you will inevitably have to change. Big things, big changes. And suddenly, fear of change pushes all your high hopes out of a very large, very high up, thirtieth-floor window.

You see, change goes against all we seek in life—comfort. Which is so ironic because, when it comes to our money, if we're willing to change and go through the process, we'll actually end up *more* comfortable than we've ever been. And that's the tension we feel when it comes to the fear of change. It's the pause we feel about sacrificing what we want *now* for what we want *most.*

Will it be worth it? is the question that keeps us up at night. The reality is that change requires, well, change. Adapting feels scary. And so, like an oatmeal cookie with raisins, we pick out the new scary parts (the raisins, obviously) and keep the cookie we're used to. Even though an oatmeal cookie isn't our first choice, sure, we'll eat it. But no way we're eating those raisins.

In this way, we mostly resign to life as we've known it.

Fear of Judgment

I mentioned earlier that my husband and I got married two weeks after college graduation. In the early days of our marriage, I worked at a men's clothing store in Nashville called Bachrach. It was situated in an upscale mall in a posh area of town, and I had worked my way up to an associate manager role—which meant that I had keys to open and close the store on my own, and I was now making $12 per hour instead of $10. Hot diggity dog!

While I was excited about my promotion, I knew what I really wanted was a job performing music. And like I mentioned in chapter 1, Sam and I had come back from our honeymoon with a plan to make that happen. In a few short months, we'd both been hired to do our dream jobs.

I knew the time was coming to let my boss, Joseph, know I'd be leaving soon. Joseph was much older than me, by thirty years or so, easily, and I enjoyed working with him. I set up a time for us to meet over our fifteen-minute break. We grabbed a bench in the center of the mall's main drag, and I told him about my exciting new endeavor. Sam and I were going to be pursuing our entertainment dreams! He was quiet until I finished.

"So, as of today, I have to put in my two weeks' notice," I concluded. What happened next totally shocked me.

"Huh," he said, crossing his arms with a skeptical look on his face. He leaned forward, adjusted his glasses on his nose, and scoffed. "You really think this is gonna be your big break? You're just gonna give up everything for this *little cruise job*? Trust me, honey, you'll be back. They always come running back."

His reaction to my success shook me. He was my elder, but was that . . . jealousy I detected? How? I was at least thirty years younger than this dude. *What in the world?* But it was. Although Joseph *usually* had a great attitude and was super friendly, it was clear to me that he wasn't happy in his career based on things I'd heard him say. Being manager at Bachrach at his age hadn't necessarily been his path of choice. And in that moment, I realized that maybe I was doing something he always wanted to do but had never done. I was stepping out and betting on myself—pushing past fears and unknowns and embracing the discomfort of change to better my life.

It wasn't the last time I encountered that sort of behavior. Over the course of the years to come, I started to notice a quality emerging in my personality. For lack of a better word, I'll call it the "shrink back." It was this tendency to make my growth and achievements smaller, to shrink back from notice, because I didn't want to make anyone else feel uncomfortable or, worse, have them think that I was all uppity now because of whatever success I was experiencing—especially when it came to financial success.

And I'll be totally honest: Joseph was someone who I expected to be proud of me. When the people we want to please, or who we want to be proud of us, are continuously unfazed or unimpressed, we tend to downplay our wins to avoid feeling hurt by their indifference (or in Joseph's case, their jealousy). Sound familiar at all? Some of you are in that same boat, but it's not with Joseph. It's your close friends, your family, your own flesh and blood—your people—who make you feel some type of way anytime you start doing right with your money. Anytime you start breaking free from what has kept the people around you stuck.

It's not only their judgment you fear; it's the added fear of what happens if you falter even a little bit. They'll be able to say those four smug little words: "I told you so!"

Or maybe they sound a bit more like my old manager:

"I told you you'd be back, honey."

"I told you your *little budget* wouldn't work."

"They always come back."

And so now you're in the clutches of a Catch-22. If you succeed, someone will judge you. If you fail, someone will judge you.

The thing we all need to understand is this: These people are haters. Yes, I know you may love them or look up to them or even respect them, but in this moment, with you and the money moves you are trying to make, they are haters—they aren't helpers.

The positive effects of getting on a plan with your money are almost impossible to hide. And you should continue regardless of what the haters may do or say. Because the truth is, sometimes when you do things that are good, responsible, and smart with your money in front of people who are making choices that are bad, irresponsible, and stupid with *their* money, it becomes a mirror, and they see the reality of the choices they are making. And instead of using it as an opportunity to evaluate their own financial choices and possibly improve them, they simply choose to take another sip of Haterade.

It's cool. To quote Mel Robbins, "Let them."

Unfortunately, when that behavior comes from our loved ones, or people we like and whose approval we seek, it can creep into our confidence and make us shrink back. We start to downgrade the importance of what we're doing or trying to do, and in some extra-toxic cases, it can make us toss our own growth and potential to the wayside for fear of how our success might affect those around us.

Take it from me, don't shrink back simply to make others feel comfortable. To loosely quote award-winning actress and producer Viola Davis: Don't set yourself on fire to keep the haters warm.

I get it—this is easier said than done. As a matter of fact, this is something I still work on to this day. Let me tell you what has helped. First off, I know who "my people" are. These are the people who are *for* me. These are people who have the "get it" factor. You can tell them you just made a million dollars—and they get it! They are truly supportive. They are so confident in who they are that your success doesn't threaten them. So you can share wins and opportunities and what you're striving for without worry of some backhanded compliment or passive aggressive "good for you!" response.

Sam and I have a buddy, Raul, and another friend, Ben, who have the "get it" factor. We can tell them anything financially, and they are genuinely happy and excited for us. I'm exceedingly grateful for them.

I also know, through therapy, who isn't for me. It's not that these people don't love or care for me, but they don't have the tools to show it in a healthy way. And if I'm guarding my heart and protecting my peace like we talked about earlier, I know I can't trust them to hold these things in the proper regard. I love them, but they aren't on the list of folks I'm celebrating with.

Having clarity on this list of supporters and haters is important. But if you ever do find yourself in a spot where someone on the "haters" list belittles your accomplishments, don't be silent—call them out. In the past, I've asked the question, "What do you mean by that?" or said, "Help me understand what you mean by that."

You could also take a page out of the Jefferson Fisher playbook. Fisher is a trial lawyer, an author, and in my opinion, an expert at managing uncomfortable conversations. He recommends asking the person to repeat the comment. Say, "Hey, could you repeat that?" Or take it a step further and ask about their intentions: "Hey, did you mean for that to sound condescending?"

This will cause the haters to stop in their tracks. Instead of you being the target, the tables are turned. They are now in *your* crosshairs. Asking these simple, direct questions will not only cause a naysayer to retreat, but it will build your confidence in the practice of defending yourself in a healthy way instead of shrinking back.

Fear of Missing Out

The kids call it FOMO, and here's what this fear comes down to at its most basic: You don't want to follow a plan for your money because you're afraid you won't be able to spend money on the things you enjoy. You don't want to increase your income by side hustling for a season because you're scared you'll miss out on fun with your friends. You don't want to take the plan's advice and live on less for a few years to get debt-free because you don't want to miss out on those family vacations.

Look, I get it. It's hard to miss out on things we enjoy or things we feel we deserve. But I think you deserve a life of freedom and peace with your money, not a life of debt and stress and fear, with the occasional fun sprinkled in. So listen, if you want to be afraid of missing out on something, be afraid of missing out on building wealth; be afraid of missing out on what it feels like to be debt-free; be afraid of missing out on paying for your daughter's wedding. It's time we reframe what we deserve and what we don't want to miss out on!

New Light

Let me show you a tactical solution that can help you in the moment fear strikes. Something I've found in my own personal money journey is that the antidote to fear is fruit.

Say what? Let me explain.

When Sam and I got serious about this Baby Steps plan, there were still several teachings that I had *issues* with. For instance, the idea that from now on we don't borrow money for cars. Honestly speaking, I felt tried. It was like that moment in Kevin Hart's *Laugh at My Pain* special. *Wait a minute! Wait a* minute, *Dave. I know you're not gonna just speed past that like you didn't just say what you just said!*

Where I came from, paying cash for cars was impossible. I didn't know anybody who'd done it. So this "no car loans" rule being part of it made me question the other things I was doing in the plan. I felt scared. I was thinking, *This Dave guy better be right! What if I'm not able to get a car in cash like he said? Not me sacrificing all this and working this hard and selling off my Hummer just to end up in debt again!*

But this was where I learned to "trust the fruit." The fruit is simply what something produces. Everything has fruit. An idea, a behavior, a habit, a relationship, even a plan for your money—it all produces an outcome that we can sum up as mostly good or mostly bad. Fruit is the proof that something is working or that it isn't working. So fruit acts as an indicator of the truth. The fruit is the straight-up facts of what came from that action or behavior (and remember, facts are our friends).

So in this case of my doubting the car teaching, I looked at the fruit: Sam and I had worked the plan so far, and it had really helped. We had $1,000 saved. We weren't using credit cards anymore. We fought less. We were making our way through this debt slowly but surely. The fruit was good. The truth was, the plan was working. I may have had fears or discomfort about some of the guidance, but those were fears of the future based on my limited experience and that of the folks around me. And if the fruit is the proof, this plan had good fruit in abundance. So when it came to my fears around not using car loans, I needed to stay the course—even when it was scary.

When you cut up that first credit card, yeah, you may feel fear. When you throw all but $1,000 of your savings on that first debt, it will feel scary. When you build a budget that cuts out many of your typical spending habits, like weekend brunch or vacations, you'll get hit with some FOMO. But after that first thirty days, you'll notice: Wow, this is the first time you've gone this long without creating more debt! *This is good.* You didn't argue with your spouse about the credit card bill. *Very good.* You actually paid off that medical bill that's been nagging at you for months. *This is great!*

This is good fruit.

Now keep in mind, fear doesn't always go away completely. But the more we see that good fruit as evidence, the more it causes our fears to displace and lose ground. So remember: Trust the fruit—the fruit is the proof!

Shadow Days

A lot of how we deal with our fears seems to be internal or done quietly. We're thinking inside our head, we're mentally running our numbers, we're deciding what we deserve, we're weighing if the change will be worth it. But this next antidote for fear can only be done out loud.

I wrote before about how Sam's and my money journey spanned seven and a half years. I don't have to tell you that a lot of life takes place in that span of time. During the earlier part of our journey, we went through loss—we both lost our grandfathers, and Sam even lost his dad.

Grief is hard. Grief with $460,000 of debt and mistakes on top is depressing. Grief, with the debt, plus the fact that it was keeping us from starting the family we wanted? Profound.

It was during this time that my biggest fear became spiraling into hopelessness and depression we couldn't emerge from. One night, as we got ready for bed, I peeked in the bathroom and saw my husband brushing his teeth. He was staring at his reflection in the mirror—but I saw in his eyes that his thoughts were a million miles away. I knew what he was doing. He was calculating. Counting the costs. And despairing. *Would we ever be free? Or did our debt ruin everything? Was it all worth it?*

I'm just gonna come out and say it: My biggest fear was that our debt would cost my husband his life. I tear up writing this because I carried this secret fear for so long. It drove me. It was the reason we *had* to win. But I was also afraid to talk about it because I thought it would make things worse. Finally, I realized this was unhealthy. *I can't live like this. This is not a fear I need or want.* I had to tell him what I was afraid of—that my deepest, darkest financial fear, in the end, had nothing to do with money.

I had to say it out loud.

Much like the infamous "Pull the car over!" moment, this was a moment that needed to happen, and we were both better for it. Sam and I were able to talk openly about our emotions and fears. What was in the dark, torturing us, came out into the light. And suddenly I realized my fear, though rational, no longer held the power it once did. And we could work together to build on the truth.

I realized in that season that fear loves to be a deep dark secret. Because that's when it's strongest. But when light shines in the darkness, the darkness cannot overcome it.

The truth is, money holds a lot of fears. Some of them are more surface-level, comfort-related fears like I talked about earlier in the chapter. But many of them are deep, trauma-related fears connected to our past or our own complex history with money and relationships. I'm here to remind you to deal with both. And the latter almost always requires saying it out loud, not just to a spouse or loved one, but often to a counselor or mental-health professional.

Belief

We've just talked about getting our fears out of our head and into the open. But there is also a very real solution to our fear that begins on the *inside*. So let's look at addressing our fears from a more philosophical point of view. It's time to think about what we think about.

I believe there's some powerful wisdom and insight in the Bible about who we are as people, what we're capable of when it comes to our thoughts, and how those thoughts can impact our emotions. That insight can be extremely tactical and affirming for a journey like this!

Remember when I mentioned that we were not given a spirit of fear but a spirit of power, love, and self-control? Listen, that's a pretty sweet identity to own. Knowing that I may experience fear, but it's *not* who I am and *doesn't* define who I was created to be, is freeing. Come on, somebody! The same is true for you—you literally have the power baked inside of you to exercise self-control and to push back the financial fears that are trying to hold you back. That's a sweet deal.

So how do we put this into action? When you find yourself dwelling on fearful thoughts, you have to stop and challenge them. I love how 2 Corinthians 2:5 talks about this concept—it says, "We take captive every thought to make it obedient to Christ" (NIV). It's important to know that Christ is synonymous with the truth. So this essentially doubles down on the idea that we have power when it comes to our thoughts. We can "grab" our fearful thoughts that don't line up with what's true and call them out!

And once we have that negative thought running for the hills, we must replace it with something new that is both true and helpful. And when we do that, we're literally transforming our mind. We're doing exactly what Romans 12:2 says: "Be transformed by the renewing of your mind" (NIV).

So stop now and take time to do just that. Use the space provided, or grab a journal, and work through the following prompts.

FACE AND REPLACE YOUR FEARS

1. First, write down the fearful thought.

Example: *I'm afraid I'll alienate my friends and family by sticking to my budget.*

____

____

____

2. Next, answer the question: Is this actually true? (Is this a fact?)

Example: *I honestly don't know if it will alienate them. I guess I'd have to ask them to truly know.* Or *Yes, I've tried before, and it has made my friends and family get weird.*

____

____

____

3. Now, replace the statement with what is true.

Example: *The reality is, no matter how my family and friends react, it's my money and my life. I control my actions. It's not my responsibility to control what someone else might think or how they might act.*

____

____

____

Remember, our fears could be based on beliefs that are rational or irrational and threats that are real or imagined. It's possible that you'll notice your fear is based on something real and true. But it doesn't change the exercise. You can still replace a real, legitimate fear that's been holding you back with another truth that will help you move forward. Just like we did in the example.

Sure, fear may be the explanation to the way you were thinking about money before, but those fearful thoughts don't have to define what you do next. If I hid a box in your attic but never told you about it, you'd never go looking for it—and you'd probably never find it by chance either. But if I told you, "Hey, I put a box in your attic. It's yours," you'd be curious. And if I told you, "Hey, I put a box in your attic. It's yours, and there's a treasure inside," you would then feel compelled to go look for it so that you could access what's inside.

The point is, this power of exchanging our thoughts is a treasure. It's a valuable tool for making progress in your life and with your money. But this power isn't obvious. It requires digging deep inside to find it. You may not have even known it was there. But now that you know it's there, you can be intentional to find it and use it. And when you do, you'll finally have the ability to change your behavior to get your spending under control, to accept the parameters of a plan for your money, or to maintain the self-control to stick to a monthly budget, no matter which fears try to slow you down.

Crossroads

Wait a minute. It seems like we spent an awful lot of time talking about the if-I-do-this-plan fears. But now, let's flip the script and spend some time unpacking a more rational and more scary set of fears. I'm talking about the if-I-*don't*-do-this-plan fears.

Did you know that fear can keep you in a place that is actually scarier than the thing you're scared to do?

You're scared of getting on a budget and getting rid of cable and extras for two years while you pay off debt—so instead, that $100,000 of student loan debt you've been carrying continues to grow and continues to cut into what you can put away for retirement.

You're scared of what your friends and family might think if they see you sell your newer vehicle for a cash clunker and find out you're delivering Instacart as a side hustle to get your loans paid off—so instead, you put your home at risk and roll all your debt into your mortgage. Meaning, if you lose your job and it takes a while to get back to your old salary, or there's a dip in the housing market, you could find yourself upside-down on your home or stuck with a payment that's suddenly a lot harder to afford.

Don't let fear keep you in a place that's scarier than the thing you're scared to do. You need to be asking yourself, *If I don't do this plan—if I don't get my money under control—what is there to fear?* Or put another way: *What do I stand to lose?*

You have to know what's at stake in order to push past your fears. For Sam and me, it felt like *everything* was at stake. No-brainer. But what's at stake for you? What's the vision you have for your life that is at risk if nothing changes?

Take a moment and really think about that.

Again, that's what I loved about the movie *The Pursuit of Happyness*. Gardner starts out in a paycheck-to-paycheck situation, with an unstable, unsustainable business and in an unhealthy relationship. But once he gets hold of a vision for a better life, and he has a plan to get there, suddenly his vision for the future is on the line. Everything is at stake! He *has* to work the plan successfully in order to obtain his goal. He can tell himself there's no guarantee this will work. Or he can tell himself *he* is the guarantee this will work.

We have to tell ourselves the same because what's at stake is the life that we really want deep down inside. We want the house with the big kitchen island. We want a job that we love. We want to start that business. We want to see six figures in an account that's all ours. We want to feel more secure in our marriage. We want to feel peace and freedom. And it should be scarier to think that if we don't change, if we don't get on a plan, we'll be locked into debt and stress forever.

Just like *The Pursuit of Happyness* shows, if you want something, you have to go get it. You have to pursue it, you have to chase it—and you can't let fear stop you.

So exchange the unhelpful, fearful thoughts with helpful, truthful thoughts and move forward. Because the more you move forward, the more fruit you will begin to see. And when you start to see that fruit—the proof that *this is working*—it gives you hope and confidence to continue. The resulting hope and confidence will start to displace those old, unhelpful fears.

And remember, the only fear you need to hold tight to is the healthy fear that lights the fear under your butt: *What happens if I don't do it?*

CHAPTER SEVEN

GUILT AND SHAME

Avalanche

When Sam and I first got married, I knew he had student loans. But I had no idea exactly how much—and neither did he. We knew it was probably a decent amount, considering he'd gone to Berklee College of Music and University of Miami and then finished out at Tennessee State University. When we finally realized the loans had started around $200,000 and had grown closer to $230,000 with interest, we were flabbergasted. His loans plus my own $34,000 felt like an unbearable weight. Out of all our debt, this was the hardest mountain to climb.

"Mine" were less and were broken into smaller chunks, so they were (comparatively) easier to knock out with the Debt Snowball. "Sam's" were . . . well, a lot. Now I *never* faulted Sam for the debt he brought into the relationship. I was never mad at him for it, and I certainly never resented him. In my mind, we were married—for better or worse. His debt was my debt, and vice versa. It was the same with our income. We were one. But I did have questions, like, how did this happen?

For Sam, like so many other college students, the plan was to chase his dreams and go to his dream school—whatever the cost. "Student loans can help you!" he was told. After all, "They're good debt!" So that's what he did. And to make things even more messy, Sam's mom cosigned most of the debt, which meant that she was like the third wheel when it came to finances in our marriage. And I honestly don't blame her, because every move we made directly affected her.

I don't have to tell you—it was stressful. And I could tell Sam carried a lot of guilt and embarrassment that this series of choices was continuously wedging itself into our lives.

Then there was the other part. Not only was Sam feeling the heat of his mom wanting him to get those loans paid, but he was also feeling the weight of the reality that we were putting our own family on hold to get those loans paid. The clock was ticking on our plans to one day have a child of our own.

Now let me be clear. The Baby Steps don't say you have to wait until you're debt-free to have children. *We* decided that we wanted financial stability before we took that step. We had a clear picture of the life we wanted to create, and if that meant waiting, then so be it. But all this pressure ultimately did a number on Sam. He carried so much guilt and regret over his portion of student loans and the negative effect it was having on our marriage and his relationship with his mom.

That guilt played out in a laundry list of different ways. I noticed Sam became overly defensive in day-to-day matters, even beyond the money stuff. He was always in his head, retreating from direct questions—and not just with me. I observed he was always avoiding calls and conversations with his mom, not just about money but any- and everything.

The guilt was also creating a weird competition in his mind between him and me. It seemed like he was trying to prove to me all the things he could do "right" and "good." But I didn't need convincing—I knew exactly the man he was, and his past mistakes never sullied the way I viewed him. If anything, I viewed him as an even stronger, more courageous, more hard-working leader who would stop at nothing to make this right. He was right there with me, leading the charge to a better life for our family. But despite my belief and my pep talks, even in our happiest moments, I could still see that the guilt and sadness wouldn't let him go. His eyes always betrayed the guilt and pain he was feeling.

The guilt was building up all these walls, as if closing himself off was a way to protect himself. And opening up would mean having to face the guilt and acknowledge the magnitude of how his choices (no matter how well-intended or ill-informed) had affected not just himself but others.

I Wish

At the lowest level, we've all made a stupid, impulsive choice with our money and later wished we hadn't done it. That's what I'd call regret—feeling bad about a choice and wishing we had done something different. Usually, it's something that was done in the past out of financial ignorance that is now causing very present pain. This is the root of good, old-fashioned buyer's remorse.

"I can't believe I let that salesman talk me into that green velvet furniture set with zero payments until 3030."

"I can't believe I let that salesman talk me into buying solar panels here in Seattle. I wasn't even in the market for them!"

It's one of the reasons I hate credit cards—you're always living in past regret when it comes time to pay the bill. You're left with that I-could-kick-myself feeling. *Why'd I buy that stupid dress? Why'd I put those Jordans on credit?* That's why they call interest APR—it's added pain and regret.

In my opinion, this type of regret is that first layer of *What was I thinking?* before the pain of straight-up guilt. As long as it doesn't affect anyone else, we usually can get away with just that sheepish feeling of remorse. But I find that once other people's lives get involved, the feeling quickly gets a lot deeper and turns into all-out guilt.

Guilt: *The sense of regret and fault we feel*
when our decisions have an unfavorable impact
(real or perceived) on someone else.

So how do guilt and regret differ? Let me paint you a picture. While hosting *The Ramsey Show* recently, I talked to a guy named Justin. He had cosigned a car loan with his girlfriend and was on the hook for more than $25,000. And guess what? Just a few weeks after he signed, they broke up. Now she's just somebody that he used to know—and somebody whose debt he's tangled up in. The relationship with her is over, but he's still in a relationship with her new car loan.

"What can I do?" he asked, with an edge of panic in his voice.

"Unfortunately, not much," I say. "You could ask her to refinance the loan, but that's likely impossible. She clearly won't qualify on her own; otherwise she wouldn't have needed a cosigner."

I could feel the disappointment on the other line, but I kept delivering the bad news.

"All you can do is hope she pays it off and, in the meantime, stack up a pile of money to the side in case she decides to go MIA and you have to pay this whole thing."

"But I have debt of my own!" he protested.

"Yeah, and, unfortunately, now this is part of it," I sighed. "Sorry, my guy, and thanks for the call."

I felt bad for Justin. He was feeling a lot of regret about the situation. I could tell he wished he'd made a better decision. His now-ex-girlfriend, however, will likely have to deal with guilt because her decision to include him in this mess is causing him to experience a negative (and potentially expensive) outcome. And financial guilt, my friends, can be a doozy if you don't deal with it.

Shoulda, Woulda, Coulda

I find time and time again that guilt is one of the biggest emotional barriers that people face when they are trying to get their money on track. Look back at that definition in the last section. Guilt is that knot we get in our stomach when our choices lead to negative outcomes for ourselves, yes, but even more so when those negative outcomes extend to someone else. Especially the people we love. I mean, it's virtually impossible to talk about money without experiencing that "shoulda, woulda, coulda" pang of guilt and feeling the weight of all those unmet expectations (real or perceived) that sit on our shoulders.

I find that financial guilt is usually a result of one of two circumstances: something we *did* or something we *didn't* do. Let's start by looking at when guilt pops up because of something we did.

On a different day hosting *The Ramsey Show,* I took a call from a guy who'd always earned a good income, but when he lost his job, his family fell on hard times and he turned to credit cards. He'd always been the one who handled the finances in the marriage, and he didn't want his wife to worry. So he racked up over $50,000 of credit card debt just trying to stay afloat—and his wife was none the wiser. He kept assuring her that things were fine, until she finally discovered the debt. He was riddled with guilt over losing his job, going into debt, and then lying about it.

I talked to a young lady named Bethany even more recently who was ready to get her money under control, but she was stuck. Bethany wanted to work extra overtime hours, but she lived with her mom and grandmother and was trying to figure out how she could explain the extra time at work. When I pressed her further about why she couldn't simply say, "I'm working to get out of debt," she began to cry. It turns out, the more than $30,000 of debt she was working to pay off came from a previous relationship where her boyfriend had taken advantage of her financially and run up debt under her name. Bethany explained that she had been raised "better than that" and that her parents had shown her good money principles. It turned out that she was so ashamed and felt so guilty about the debt, the thought of explaining to her family that she'd gotten into this mess brought her to tears. The guilt she was carrying was holding her back from taking on the overtime hours she needed, and something had to change.

I hear these kinds of stories time and time again: The spouse who had a season of online addiction to gambling, shopping, or worse—and they've come clean, but the guilt and consequences of their mistakes continue to weigh on them and their relationships. Or the guy who got a raise and, out of excitement, bought a brand-new truck with a monthly payment of more than $800. Next thing he knows, his wife (who warned him not to get the truck in the first place) is pregnant and no longer working—and that truck payment has them upside-down.

Mistakes are painful enough when *we* have to deal with the consequences, but they really fill us with guilt when others get the short end of the stick. Whether it's the feeling of having let down the parents who "raised us better than that" or the spouse who was counting on us to "take care of the finances," financial guilt of "what we did" can really do a number on us. Yes, it can hold us back from moving forward with our money, but even worse, it can hold us back from connecting with the people who love us most.

Never Enough

Other times, our guilt is tied to something we didn't do or aren't yet able to do.

I'll never forget years ago when Sam and I were in the throes of our debt-free journey; we'd let go of our roommates and were living in the townhouse on our own. We were budgeting and making progress, but money was still really tight. We were throwing every single extra dollar we had onto debt. But the nature of our work was very much feast or famine. We'd do a gig and put all the money on bills and debt, but sometimes we'd be waiting for weeks before we'd work again. We'd grown accustomed to living for lengthy spans with little to no money in our account. We were still navigating how to plan for the fluctuations in our income while being intense about paying off debt. During those days, we survived on income from side hustles until our next big gig. Once during one of the two- to three-week spans when our account was basically at zero (and I'm not exaggerating—there was less than $10 in our account), I got a call.

It was my sister.

Her family had all taken a trip to Orlando for vacation, and she'd had a medical emergency while they were enjoying one of the theme parks. She was in the hospital, and they were trying to figure out what was wrong.

Now you need to understand that my sister is my rock, and I still get emotional thinking about this moment. She's seven years older than me and everything you could ever want in a sister. She has always been the person I look up to most—my best friend, role model, guide, and the voice of reason in my life. *Nothing* can happen to Farra. When I got the call that she was in the hospital, about a four-hour drive from where Sam and I lived, my first thought was, *I have to go! I have to get there to see her.*

But there was one glaring problem: We didn't have the money. And I mean *none*. Even if I slept in my car instead of a hotel and brought food from home, there was still the issue of gas. It was impossible. The thing is, of everyone in my family, I was by far the closest to where she was in Orlando. It seemed natural to go see her. I don't think I've ever been more embarrassed, or felt more guilty or ashamed of our situation, than I did in that moment.

And it gets worse. Listen, guilt will make you do weird things. I wanted gas money, but I didn't want to admit to my parents that we had absolutely no cash (the result of working the plan out of order with no emergency fund). So I called my dad and made up some weird lie—I don't even remember the details of what I told him—but it was a ploy to get him to send me $100. He did.

But you see, back then we didn't have conveniences like Venmo. If someone sent you money, it still took a couple days for you to actually get it. Of course, I should have considered that before lying because by the time the money got to me, the emergency would likely be over. And in that time, Sam or I would have been able to do a music lesson or something else to get some cash quickly. But I was at the bottom of the barrel. I wasn't thinking straight. I felt unbearably guilty, and I was desperate.

I felt like Julia Roberts' character, Julianne, in *My Best Friend's Wedding*, when she tearfully admits her actions.

"I'm pond scum," she chokes out. "Lower, actually. I'm like the fungus that feeds on pond scum."

"Lower," Dermot Mulroney's character, Michael—the best friend whose wedding she's been trying to sabotage—interjects.

"The puss, that infects the mucus, that cruds up the fungus, that feeds on the pond scum."

Now in the next moment, he thanks her for loving him that much. And, spoiler alert, the wedding goes on. But really, she was beating herself up at this point.

I felt all that and more. This wasn't about something I'd done but what I *couldn't* do for Farra.

What kind of sister was I?

The guilt of not being able to show up when my family needed me most because I didn't have *gas money* was like a throat punch. And to make matters worse, rather than reach out honestly for help, I'd lied about it.

The truth is, our debt-free journey was riddled with moments where our money situation caused me guilt and regret for the moment. But as tough as it was, Sam and I always found a way to convert that awful feeling into fuel. The mantra became: *We never want to be in this situation again.*

99 Problems

"What about me, Jade? I'm doing right, but I still feel wrong!"

I'll tell you right now, this third variety of guilt is real. It's not that you did something wrong with money or that you didn't do something right . . . you feel guilty about doing the *right* thing. So many of us feel guilty because we feel like we could have "shown up" for someone we love financially but chose not to because we were trying to make wise decisions.

Do any of these situations callers of *The Ramsey Show* have shared sound familiar?

- A son tells me he feels obligated to take care of aging parents who were irresponsible with their money. But he's trying to take care of his own immediate family and doesn't have the margin to assist.
- A girl says her boyfriend wants her to cosign a loan with him for a vehicle, but she knows it's a bad idea and says no.
- A parent is considering taking out a Parent PLUS loan for their daughter, who wants to attend a certain school that's clearly out of the family's price range, but they know debt isn't the answer.
- A guy tells me he's feeling guilty about asking his uncle, who has been mooching off the family's inherited property, to move out.

These folks feel bad about standing their ground and not enabling bad financial behavior. Plus, they've got their own financial problems, and they don't need to add someone else's to the pile.

A few years ago, I was hosting a webinar where folks who were working the Baby Steps and learning to budget could join virtually to ask their questions and get free coaching. Toward the end of the webinar, a young lady raised her hand to ask a question. Her slightly fuzzy image came up on the Zoom screen, and she began to share her situation. She was a single mom with two kids, living paycheck-to-paycheck, with a car that was worth less than she owed and a payment that had her in a chokehold. Plus, her rent was eating up too much of her take-home pay. She had a larger apartment than she really needed so that her kids could have separate rooms and her mother could live with them. And ultimately, her salary just wasn't enough to make ends meet.

My advice to her wasn't surprising: She needed to downsize to a smaller apartment, meaning Mom would need to move out and the kids would need to share a room. She also needed to sell the upside-down car and use the cash she had to buy a $5,000 beater to get around. And finally, she needed to get her income up—start applying for jobs that paid more and work more hours in the meantime.

She admitted she already knew this was the *logical* answer. But she shared with the group that guilt was holding her back. She felt guilty for making her kids share a room at their age because they wanted to have their own space. The idea of working more hours and taking time away from her children brought on a whole new wave of mom guilt. She felt bad asking her mom to move out. And the fact that her car payment (a bad decision on her part) was one of the many factors keeping their backs against the wall each month just added to the pile. Her guilt was not just keeping her in financial chaos; it was also putting her in a position to end up resenting her mom and kids down the road.

The good news is, despite her misgivings, she actually followed my advice! Months later she joined another webinar to share the update that she moved apartments, sold her car, and got a better-paying job. Her financial life was finally moving in the right direction! In hindsight, she realized that her guilt had created a crazy cycle that was keeping her stuck. You've probably seen this in your own life at some point too.

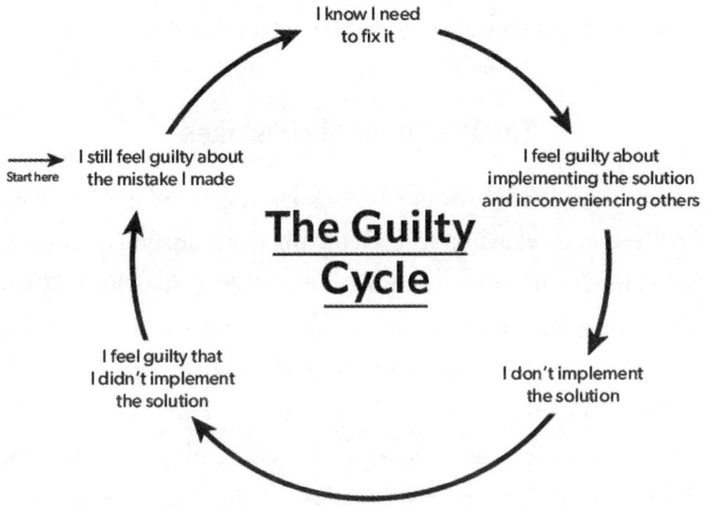

These moments hit different because you feel bad about doing what's right, even though you *know* it's the right move. Usually, this comes from an expectation that you believe someone else has of you that you won't meet. In this way, it can feel similar to the guilt that focuses on "what you didn't do." But there's a key difference. Instead of being limited by your circumstances for something you wish you *could* do for someone, in this case, you're *choosing*, from a place of intelligence and a level head, not to make a bad financial decision. You don't want to disappoint anyone, but if you were to dig deep, you know giving in would be the wrong move for all parties involved. You know cosigning a loan is dumb. You know taking on student loans for your child can become a relationship landmine down the road. But you love the person who is asking this of you, and you feel obligated, so you find yourself considering making a bad decision.

The Weight of My Mistakes

I talked earlier about how our actions are directly affected by what we believe and what we feel. Remember, if behavior is the car, belief is in the driver's seat, and emotions steer the wheel. When it comes to guilt, I find that many times it steers us to rationalize our behavior, therefore we never go in the right direction. It's like a coping mechanism. Because having to admit we were wrong or that we let someone down is the *worst*. As a result of that, we tend to rationalize that mistake we made—or the one we're about to make. Have you done this? I know I have.

When Sam and I were in credit card debt, I felt *so* guilty. At one point, we had *fourteen* credit cards—all completely maxed out. To cope, I told myself we didn't have a choice. How else were we supposed to afford the things we needed? I was so busy rationalizing to avoid that sense of guilt that I couldn't accept the truth and actually do something about the situation. It wasn't until I owned the truth and stopped making excuses that we were able to make a real change. We were the ones making the choice to use credit cards. And if we wanted to stop, we could.

Similarly, a guy named Andre called into the show from St. Louis, Missouri. Andre was a dude in his early twenties who'd grown up on welfare and in government housing most of his life.

His mom was a single parent, and she didn't work much for fear of losing her welfare. This young man loved his mom but was showing it all wrong. Andre had moved out, but his younger brother was still living at home. He told me he was trying to help his mom with the budget and teach her the Baby Steps but wasn't getting very far. So Andre was giving all of his money to pay her bills and take care of his little brother.

When he called, he was considering buying a house with his mom out of pure guilt. He rationalized it by saying things like, "She took care of me, so I feel I need to take care of her." I tried to convince him of the foolishness in this idea. While his heart was in the right place, he was setting fire to his own finances to save someone who didn't want to be saved. When it came down to it, he felt guilty that he was finally able to move beyond welfare and that his mom wasn't going forward with him. Andre's guilt was causing him to rationalize a string of bad financial choices.

I had to remind him of the cold hard truth: His mom is an adult. She makes her own choices. That means she is the only one accountable for them—and making a change is up to her too. I went on to tell Andre that he was a good son, with good (albeit misguided) intentions. I told him I thought it would be wonderful if he helped make sure his brother was cared for because he was still younger. But Andre had to accept that his mother was making her own bed to lay in.

I won't lie—these are some of the hardest calls I take. The reality is that, sometimes, the people we love most want us to enable their bad behavior with money. When it comes to loved ones, so much of money is not just about money—it's about healthy boundaries. When we don't have healthy boundaries in place, we open ourselves up to catastrophic money mistakes. And if we're not careful, we will rationalize intentionally going forward with a bad choice out of guilt and misdirected love for them.

Sinking Deep

Have you ever noticed that, after a while, guilt can start to mess with your confidence? It can start to mess with your sense of self. You think, *If I made a mistake like that, how can I trust myself to make the right choices?* And if you're married, you might think, *Dang, why should my spouse trust my judgment?*

I once heard someone say, "Emotions are meant to go through us. Problems start when our feelings get stuck." When we get stuck in guilt rather than letting it go through us, it can morph into another unhelpful emotion: shame.

Shame: *The feeling that our poor decisions are our identity.*

I'm a screw-up.
I'm just bad at money.
I'm careless and irresponsible.
I'm just a hot mess.
I'm ruining his life.
I'm ruining her life.
If it weren't for me, we'd be further ahead.

When Sam and I were going through our student loan drama, I remember hearing Sam say things like this: "I feel like I'm ruining your life," "I'm slowing you down," and "I hate being the reason we can't start a family."

I knew that was the emotions talking, but it bothered me because I knew it was deeper than guilt. What I heard sounded like shame. Guilt is when you feel bad about the thing you did and the results of it. Shame is when that choice becomes your identity. In your mind, it's no longer that you *made* the mistake. You start to believe you *are* the mistake. You are the failure. You are the problem.

You can see why this is a dangerous emotion to ignore.

If you've ever said things like this about yourself, I want to remind you, there's a difference between you and the mistake you made. You took the student loan debt. But *the debt* is the problem, not you. You invested in a bad business plan. You aren't bad—the business plan was. You made a mistake. And while it's important to own your mistakes, it's also incredibly important to remember that *you are not the mistake.*

Now that you know the truth of the situation, you can begin to see what the real enemy is, and it's not you.

Look What You Made Me Do

While guilt can cause us to rationalize our choices, over time I've seen that shame causes a different reaction within us. Since shame makes us feel like we *are* the mistake—when our choice becomes our identity—the result is often a feeling of self-loathing. In our heads, we've become the problem, and that can be hard to bear. So as a coping mechanism, we start pointing that finger away from us and at anyone and everyone else.

I for sure spent time blaming folks—it couldn't just be me on the hook! I had to make sure to name and point at every person or thing that had any sort of role in our money mess. And that included but was not limited to . . .

- The lady in the financial aid office who suggested I take on debt. (That was terrible advice!)
- The student loan companies. (How could they be so careless to give these loans to kids?)
- Our parents. (How could they let us sign up for this? Why didn't they stop us?)

I was blaming everyone and their mama! Sam was too. Real talk? It's human nature to look outward to figure out exactly who's to blame for the mess you're in. If the government could get inflation under control, you'd be able to make headway. If your spouse would just be *better* at this money stuff, you wouldn't have all these problems. If your boss had given you that raise you deserved, your debt payments wouldn't be such a strain. So you just need to wait for *them* to get their freaking act together and your life can improve, right? Wrong.

And if you're someone who's feeling guilty about what you *didn't* do, guess who you're blaming? You. You think it's your fault that your parents will struggle in retirement if you don't spot them cash every month—cash you don't have because you're trying to take care of your own situation. Weirdly enough, you blame yourself because you'd feel *guilty* for blaming your parents, even though their financial situation is their responsibility. So you point that blame back at yourself and, essentially, spiral.

We tend to feel like assigning blame—naming the guilty party—will help the situation. But here's the truth: The only thing all this blaming does is give us an excuse to stay stuck.

See, I was about two years into my blaming routine when someone finally got my attention. It was a typical Sunday morning at church, and I was sitting in the middle of the congregation when I heard Pastor David Hughes say, "You can't blame your way to a better life."

Then he paused for it to sink in.

It was like a punch in the face. Um, since when was my pastor a professional boxer? *Sheesh!* His words hit me square in the nose—and boy, did it hurt. Surely he didn't realize that Sam and I had over $460,000 of debt that we were working to pay off.

My mind tried to go into its typical routine . . . But this time, in the midst of my blissful blaming binge, his words kept reverberating in my mind: "Okay, you can't blame your way to a better life."

I said to myself, "So what are you going to do?"

And deep inside, I knew the answer. I had to choose to take control of my life and my money and quit making excuses. I knew that no matter what I'm feeling guilty about, complaining about, or ashamed about, the truth is, I can do something about it. I recognized blaming won't get me anywhere. And guess what? It won't get you anywhere either. If I could move on, so can you. And *that* is good news. That is hope.

Human

Given everything I've shared up to this point, you may be surprised when I say guilt isn't all bad. Hear me out.

If you feel that shot of guilt, that moment of feeling bad about a choice you made, that's a good thing! That means you're a person with a pulse, a working soul, and a conscience. It's a sign that you know right from wrong, good from bad, and smart from dumb. But remember, emotions are meant to pass through us. It's when we get stuck in this feeling of guilt that it causes more problems with our money.

It's meant to be a jolt to get us back on the right track or to teach us a lesson. It's like touching a hot stove—you feel that searing burn and take care never to do that again! And the worse the burn, the longer the pain can last. But that's normal. That's human. But when the sting of guilt lingers far too long and leaves you justifying more bad choices or feeling shameful, that's how we know it's high time to shake it loose.

Listen, we're humans. We make mistakes. The goal is to learn from them and move on.

Love's Divine

"Your advice is to just 'move on'? Jade, you're making this sound way easier than it is."

I know.

I've been saying this whole time that emotions aren't a light switch. It's no different here. But the best way to *begin* to move on is to embrace two things: healthy boundaries and forgiveness.

Boundaries are a way to love yourself and others well. They can give you the space you need to process and heal. And it's important to remember that boundaries shouldn't be created as a form of punishment or consequence. Instead, think of them as a protective measure to keep the people you love most, including yourself, in the safest, healthiest, and most secure place, where everyone can thrive.

Earlier in the chapter, I briefly mentioned setting proper boundaries and expectations with entitled loved ones. All that means is that you let them know up front that you love them, but you aren't willing to fund their mistakes—especially if you're already busy paying for your own. Now this doesn't have to be some long, drawn-out thing. You can simply say, "I'm not going to do that. I don't feel like it's wise for either of us." Then politely move on and change the subject.

Or this can look like informing a family member who's always bringing up the past: "Hey, whenever we talk on the phone, we end up talking about that mistake I made a long time ago. I've made peace with it, and I don't need to keep rehashing it. I'd appreciate it if we removed that from our topic list. And if it's something you need to bring up, I just want you to know I'll likely end our conversation pretty quickly."

You can even reinforce that boundary by using the Jefferson Fisher technique we used earlier. "Hey, are you trying to hurt me with that comment?" and I'd add, "If you are, I forgive you—but I'm also gonna end this conversation."

There are even boundaries you need to set for yourself. And a lot of times, they have to do with you saying enough is enough—*I've beaten myself up about this for years, and this is where I draw the line.*

This leads me to the second thing to embrace when working through guilt: forgiveness. Learning to forgive yourself for the mistakes you've made with money, or for the fact that you weren't there when someone needed you, is pivotal. As a matter of fact, in most cases, the antidote to guilt and shame with your money *is* forgiveness. And let me be clear: It's not someone else forgiving you. It's *you* forgiving yourself.

Forgiveness brings a level of peace, and the truth is, it's hard to let guilt or shame move through you until you've made peace with the mistakes you've made. One of my favorite podcasters said that God doesn't do shame, He doesn't do guilt, and He doesn't do "making you feel bad." But what God *does* bring about is conviction.

Guilt and shame, on the other hand, bring condemnation. Feeling condemned keeps us stuck. But feeling that conviction brings awareness. I'm not talking about conviction like in some courtroom drama, where someone is convicted of a crime. The type of conviction I'm talking about is that flicker of awareness, that flicker of realizing, *Oops, I shouldn't have done that.* Conviction is not only when we see the error of our ways but also when we're inspired to choose ownership of our actions. It shows us how our actions have gotten off track and paves the way for forgiveness, reconciliation, and freedom.

Ultimately, the purpose of conviction is to get us to change direction or course correct, and just like the hot stove, take care never to do that again. Conviction should not make us feel stuck or like there's something wrong with us. It should help us turn and keep moving in a better direction. It's a very normal and necessary driver of life change. It's how we grow, and it's how we become the best version of ourselves, even when it comes to finances.

Like I said before, taking out debt is not a sin, and *most* of the bad choices we made with our money aren't either—they're just mistakes.

And for me, if I'm struggling to forgive myself for a money mistake—or truly any mistake I've made—I remember this verse: "If we confess our sins, He is faithful and just to forgive us our sins and cleanse us from everything we've done wrong" (1 John 1:9 CEB). There is another verse that goes on to say that God is so forgiving that, when we go to Him with our mistakes, He's compassionate. It says our mistakes are cast as far from us "as the east is from the west"—the sunrise to the sunset (Psalm 103:12 NIV).

So you know what goes on in my head when I read that verse? *Hold on, let me get this straight! If the God of the universe can forgive me for everything I've ever done wrong (a pretty big deal), then surely, I can show myself a little compassion and forgive myself for simply making a mistake with my money (not nearly as big a deal)!*

You can do this too. When that flash of conviction opens your eyes to your mistakes, don't ignore it—acknowledge it. Because forgiveness is on the other side. When you have forgiveness, you're finally free to put down that heavy weight of guilt and shame you've been carrying, and you'll be freed up to move a lot faster and feel a lot lighter in this process.

My husband, Sam, has a great tactical method for practicing this concept of self-forgiveness: daily affirmations. But he doesn't just say them. He posts them on sticky notes all over his bathroom mirror so he can see them too. These are phrases that help him let go of guilt or mistakes and be confident of who he is today, in this moment. Words have power, especially when you repeat them daily. So today, try it yourself. Make your own sticky note that says, "I am not my mistakes. I am moving forward. I am forgiven." Put this on your bathroom mirror and say it in the morning when you get ready and in the evening when you are winding down for the night.

Now, forgiving ourselves doesn't usually happen in a flash. It's a process. It's an ongoing choice. And part of the reason it's so hard is, everything I'm talking about in this chapter is taking place upstairs, in our head. It can feel difficult just to pinpoint how we feel, who we're blaming, and what we're rationalizing with everything that's swarming around in our brain—much less get to the point of forgiving ourselves. That's why taking the time to get things down on paper can bring so much clarity. So let's do that now.

I want you to take some time to fill in the following exercise so you can see the pattern you've created. You'll be able to see the excuses and rationalizations you've made; you'll be able to fill in how shame has made you feel and who you are blaming for it. Then we'll be able to get about the work of moving through it to a place of forgiveness. This is not a quick fix—but it will help you get there faster.

PROCESSING YOUR GUILT

This worksheet will help you visualize what's going on with your feelings of guilt—so you can start to work through them in a productive way.

1. The Starting Point: What I Did or What I Didn't Do

Every experience of guilt begins with either an action we've taken or something we've left undone. Here's a chance to put on paper the thing or things that you did (or didn't do) that are creating all this drama. Write down the first actions or inactions that come to mind when you think of your money situation.

Things I did or didn't do:

____

____

____

2. Recognize Guilt and Rationalization

When we think of those things we did or didn't do, regret is usually the first emotion we feel, and it's focused inward. It's when you find yourself thinking, *Shoot, I wish I hadn't done that.* But the next layer is guilt. This is when we start to realize that our choice is having negative effects on other people in our life. And this signals a conflict with our personal values—we feel like we actually did something wrong or skipped out on being responsible. Yikes, that hurts! Often at this point, we start to rationalize our choices and make excuses as a coping mechanism. *Everyone does it*, we tell ourselves. *I didn't have any other option!* Take a moment and think back on some of the excuses you've made to yourself or to others. Write them below.

Excuses I've made:

(Examples: A student loan was the only way I could pay for college. I *needed* that new car!)

____

____

____

3. Beat Shame and Blame

Uh oh, now the narrative can begin to shift from "I did something wrong" to "I am the problem." Shame is a battle we fight on the inside—and it can be damaging to our self-esteem and our relationships if we don't address it. So, don't let these thoughts go unchallenged. Write them down below so you can examine them, just like we learned in chapter 6 with fear. Because if we don't work through these emotions, we'll find ourselves looking for somewhere to place the weight of them through blaming. Trust me, I've done my fair share of blaming, so I can tell you—blaming doesn't actually cause change. It keeps us stuck. To make progress, let's write down and challenge those feelings of shame, and let's also be honest about where we've tried to place the blame.

Shameful "I am" statements I've believed:

(Examples: I'm just a hot mess. I'm careless and irresponsible.)

I am ______________________________

I am ______________________________

I am ______________________________

Who or what I've been blaming for my situation:

(Examples: loved ones, student loans, the plan for my money)

____

____

____

4. Take Responsibility

It's time to focus on the light at the end of the tunnel. By starting this worksheet, you've started the process of owning your current emotions. That's fabulous! Now, let's take it to the next level. That starts by clearly understanding your role in the situation—what's on you, what's not on you. The truth is, you may not have been fully at fault for what took place, but regardless, your life is your responsibility to own and fix. Use the lines below to write down what you are owning in your situation. Make sure these statements are based on facts. Don't include anyone but yourself here—and avoid adding any embellishment. Here's an example of what I mean by that: *My mom talked me into taking out student loans and I ruined my life—and probably my kids' lives too.* (See a better example below.) Remember, we're moving past excuses and shifting the blame. We are simply taking responsibility for our role.

My actual role in my money situation:

(Examples: I took out a car payment I knew could be too much. I signed for $35,000 of student loans I wasn't mature enough to understand—and since I ignored them, they now total $42,000.)

____

____

____

5. Practice Forgiveness and Compassion

Mistakes are a vital part of learning. And if we can learn from our mistakes, forgive ourselves, and move on, that makes us more than human—it makes us mature. Forgiving ourselves means having compassion on ourselves, just like we would for someone we love. So, we're not carrying any of that old guilt into the future! Fill in the blanks below and begin to let it go. When we write things down, they become more solid in our mind, and we're more likely to see the situation through. Think of it like a contract we're committing to.

Things I forgive myself for:

(Examples: signing up for that credit card, taking out that home equity line of credit)

____

____

____

Now, put those statements into the format below and say them out loud.

"I forgive myself for __________________________________. I accept I am human. I made a mistake."

6. Embrace a Fresh Start

Alright, my friend, it's onward and upward from here. This isn't an overnight deal, but you're going in the right direction. You're showing up each day, acknowledging the lessons you've learned and saying, "I'm no longer defined by the past. Instead, I'm dialed in on making progress." To help you with this, there are a few new "I am" statements below for you to believe. Put these daily affirmations on your mirror and make it a new daily routine to speak them out loud:

"I am not my past mistakes. I am learning. I am growing. I am moving forward. I am forgiven."

CHAPTER EIGHT

ANGER

Girl On Fire

In my history book, my thirtieth birthday will forever go down in infamy. Sam and I were spending the day in Cozumel, Mexico—one of the ports of call on the ship we were working on for that week. We'd gotten off the ship early to make the most of the day when we realized we were running low on cash. There's an area right off the ship that has tourist offices, internet cafes, restrooms, and, just what we needed, an ATM. I stopped to pull out twenty bucks in case we wanted to grab a bite to eat in port. After all, it was a milestone birthday! It was a good reason to live a little and have some fun. I noticed the ATM was giving me a few issues, and I had to try the transaction twice, but didn't think much of it. It wasn't until later, when we'd arrived at a local Starbucks to use the internet and grab something to eat, that we realized the worst had happened: Our bank account had been robbed.

When I'd used the ATM, apparently my card was skimmed. That thief had cleared out our entire account—$678 of hard-earned, much-needed income was gone. Just like that. On my birthday. I was *furious*. For a myriad of reasons! For starters—thievery. I felt completely violated. That was *our* money, and it was supposed to be safe in the bank. And this . . . *person* had taken what didn't belong to him. Next, what about my birthday? This was supposed to be a day to celebrate, but it ended up being a day fueled by anger. I spent the afternoon on the phone with a bank representative, trying to get them to understand what had happened. Which leads me to the third reason for my fury: The bank didn't buy it. The thief had taken our card info and bought $678 worth of items at the local Costco just minutes from where we were.

"Who's to say it was a thief and not you?" the bank representative's accusing voice said over the line. It was more of a statement than a question.

Ooh Lawdy! I was ready to come unglued. *Are you serious?*

"Check the time stamps!" I exclaimed. "How could I be at the ATM at 10:40 a.m. and checking out over $600 worth of stuff at Costco by 10:55 a.m. using the same card? And how would I bring all of that onto a cruise ship?"

I'd lost it. I imagined myself going through the phone and strangling that person the way Homer Simpson strangles Bart. And then the situation went from bad to worse. The bank wasn't refunding the money, so of course, the next day when our pending charges from days prior went through, they registered as overdrafted transactions, and we got hit with overdraft fees to boot. (And you all know my feelings on those dang overdraft fees!)

By the time we made it back home to sit with the manager of our bank, the account was in the red almost $1,000. I was so mad, I could've spit nails. But the bank stood firm. No refunds on ATM "fraud." Sam and I hightailed it out of there—before I made my Homer Simpson daydream a reality—and took our banking business elsewhere.

That's what I remember most about my thirtieth birthday: being angry as a snake.

They say hell hath no fury like a woman scorned, and I was living proof. If the bank was a vehicle, I was ready to take a Louisville Slugger to both headlights and dig a key into the side of that hunk of junk and drag it from here to kingdom come. I'd had it up to *here* with banks, debt collectors, budgets, credit cards, credit card payments, overdraft fees, past due payments, payment projection, missed payments, missed opportunities, missed time, and missed life.

Banks had done me wrong. Debt had played me like a fiddle.

I was beside myself.

I was angry and I was ready to be *done*.

Sam and I were in the final few years of our debt-free journey. It was the home stretch. And like any long race, I was beginning to hit a wall. But it wasn't just a wall of fatigue for me—it was a wall of sheer anger. It was starting to become clear just how much of our life and energy had been spent solving our debt problems. Sure, we were winning, but we hadn't crossed that finish line yet, and I couldn't rest until we ran under that arch. I needed to find a way to take this anger and convert it to fuel.

The truth is, anger is not a bad thing to feel. As a matter of fact, of all of the emotions that we're covering in this book, I think anger will turn out to be the most helpful and the most motivational.

Anger: *A passionate, retaliatory emotional response to perceived injustice.*

Anger is an emotional outcry for justice. Anger wants for things to be made right. Now a lot of times, we react with hostility or do things to retaliate because of anger. For this reason, many people think of it as a negative emotion—and sure, it can be. A lot of us have seen anger cause people to show the worst sides of themselves. Misdirected anger can make us belligerent and rude and combative. But anger channeled in the right direction (one that's responsive rather than retaliatory) can also be a positive and healthy catalyst to fight the good fight, and to keep pushing for change and growth. So stick with me, and I'll hash out the good, the bad, and the ugly sides of anger—and how we can move through it and use it to win and accomplish our money goals.

The Royal Scam

The thing that burns me up most is the feeling of being scammed, and I'm not just talking about some ATM thief in Mexico. I'm talking about the personal finance culture here in the United States. The problem? So much of what we've been taught about money is a scam. Think about it. From the moment we were old enough to watch TV and understand even a little bit of what the storyline and voiceovers were telling us, we were bombarded with messages that Visa was "everywhere you want to be" and American Express was so important that we should "never leave home without it."

In the same way we were told that there's "always" Coca-Cola and we should drink Gatorade if we want to "Be like Mike," we were also told that debt and credit were foundations of any solid financial life. And a lot of us bought it. Culture engrained in us that if you want success and clout, it was found in the color of your credit card and a high credit score, which is wild, considering the whole thing is a complete bust.

The credit score is marketed to sound like a necessity, but it's absolutely not. People literally made it up! Back in 1956, two guys by the name of Bill Fair and Earl Issac started Fair, Isaac and Company and spent the next two years figuring out an early algorithm to determine if someone could be "worthy to borrow money." This initial format was iterated on over the course of a few decades until, in 1989, we saw the birth of what became the modern FICO (Fair Isaac Corporation), or credit score.

Now let me be clear. The credit score measures one thing and one thing only: your relationship with debt. And there are five key factors they use to evaluate that relationship:[19]

1. How much debt you have
2. What types of debt you have
3. How long you've had your debt
4. What percentage of accessible debt you're using
5. How well you pay back your debt

Dang, that's a lot of debt. And somehow, we accepted this debt meter as our score for financial responsibility. So debt and credit became part and parcel of the adult financial experience. We take our money and give it away in payments in exchange for getting to use someone else's money. As a society, we bought the lie that it was some sort of gift or tool for us to "take advantage of." I know I did. It was great marketing.

And so, I swiped the cards, I applied for the loans, I did everything they told me I was supposed to do—and where did I end up? In $460,000 of debt with a crap credit score and nothing to show for it but a pile of bills, stress, and payments.

Oh, the humanity! Oh, the injustice of it all!

I didn't know any better, and I'm angry that I got hooked! I was told that using debt to build credit is this rite of passage. It's felt like some sort of a requirement or prerequisite to enter adulthood: I need a driver's license to operate a vehicle, and I need a good credit score to operate an adult lifestyle.

Companies bill it as a tool for independence when, really, debt is a dependence product. Make no mistake, debt is a drug, and credit is the gateway to getting addicted. And I learned this the hard way. I thought, *All I need is to build a little credit.* So I got that first store credit card, and *boom*—I was hooked. Before I knew it, I hit that high of getting what I wanted when I wanted it. More, more, more. But inevitably, the other shoe dropped, and I realized, *Shoot, I'm maxed to the limit!* The high began to wear off, but there was no more where that came from.

But trust and believe those credit companies continued to hit me up for business, only now the offers were subpar and subprime—outrageous terms and horrific interest rates. And if this rings true for you too, let me tell you: They won't stop until you stand your ground and get all Clint Eastwood and tell that gang of greedy credit vultures to "Get off my lawn!"

I experienced firsthand that, if they have their way, these companies will drain every last drop of independence and confidence you ever had to manage your hard-earned money. They'll convince you that the amount of money you make isn't good enough, so you need theirs. They'll convince you that the life your income provides isn't good enough, so they'll fund a better one. And they'll convince you that if you ever decide to stop playing their game, by their rules, you'll be penniless and exposed. They'll convince you to fear life without them in your pocket. Debt is a thief and credit is a bully—and I don't like bullies. When bullies mess with me, my friends, or my family, it makes me angry. Bullies make me want to fight back. And, well, you already know how I feel about thieves.

But I had to use my anger to fight in the right way. My response mattered. I figured out their biggest source of income is made off *my* back, when *I* pay interest and when *I* miss payments. And their whole model is based on *my* failure with money. I thought, *Wait a minute. I'm pretty integral to their whole plan working. I hold power here.*

When you've only been shown one option, it's easy to think that's all there is. We often forget that debt and credit are *products*. These big banks' and credit companies' intentions aren't to help us—it's to make a profit. The truth is, *we* don't need debt—debt needs *us*. *We* don't need credit—credit needs *us*. Without us, they are nothing.

Once I figured this out, my whole strategy changed. Instead of just being angry and hostile toward bank and credit card reps whenever I was forced to deal with them, I let my anger drive me in a more focused direction to actually do something about it: opt out. They can't make me play their game. So I decided to use all my irritation and anger and hostility to go as fast as I freaking could to pay these jokers off. Each extra payment felt like a middle finger in the face of the credit card company. And it felt good.

I began to look forward to calling in and making those extra principal payments. It felt like justice being served. I looked for more and more ways to find extra money so that I could call in and smugly say, "Yes, I'd like to make the final payment and close the account, please. I won't be doing business with you anymore." Each time a new "opportunity" for a new card came in the mail, I'd tear it up without even opening it. This felt like the retaliation I needed. I would not gratify them with my time. Once when a "You're pre-approved!" offer showed up in my mailbox, I brought it right over to the stove and turned the flame on. I burned that thing to smithereens—and it felt good. I was in control. I was using my anger to gain the upper hand.

Scream

As you can see, the implications and intentions of debt in our society fires me up. But the anger isn't always directed out there at financial corporations and big banks. We feel it at home in our daily lives.

We're angry that we're in debt.
We're angry that we have to sacrifice comfort to pay off the debt.
We're angry that we feel behind in life.
We're angry that we can't afford to go on vacation.

The list goes on and on. And to make it worse, we're not just angry at the situation; we're angry at people. We're low-key angry at our kids because they're so dadgum expensive—they need new soccer shoes and field trip money and the expensive, nut-free snacks for school. We're angry at our spouse because they don't fully get it, and they're still stopping at the gas station every day for Mountain Dew and corn nuts—plus they accidentally overdrew the account again. We're angry at our boss because we still didn't get the raise. We're angry at our coworkers because it's Janice from Accounting's birthday and "we're all chipping in for a gift." We're angry at our best friend because they planned their wedding in freaking St. Croix—now we're locked in to spend *hundreds* of bucks that we don't have because we're part of the bridal party. *Big exhale.*

It's a lot.

As Weird Al Yankovic would say, you're ready to get straight-up medieval on someone's hiney. And maybe you already have. When Sam and I were in the thick of our debt, he probably felt like he was walking on eggshells in our house. The slightest things caused me to get so angry. And to be honest, many times I took it out on him! I'd always heard that money fights and money problems were the number-one cause of divorce. And let me tell you, I've experienced firsthand why: Those were some arguments for the ages! All that anger builds up, and it's just looking for a target to be aimed at. Unfortunately, many times it's the people we love the most who get caught in our crosshairs.

The thing to remember about financial anger, especially in the context of marriage or immediate family, is this: Your loved one is not the enemy. They love you, and they're on *your* side. Let the outside source of anger be the problem, and together, you and your loved ones can all gang up against *it*. When you do this, you're pointing your anger in the right direction.

Now I know what some of you might be thinking: *If only it were that simple.* In some extreme cases, your spouse isn't helping you gang up on the problem; they are full-sail participating in the problem. You *are* angry with your spouse, and you have good reason—they have created an unsafe living situation! Let's talk about that for a minute. If your spouse is abusive in any way, or has any sort of addictions that bleed over into your money, I'm waving a red flag. He or she needs restricted access to the money.

If your spouse has been straight-up lying to you about money by hiding big purchases or debt—virtually carrying on a secret financial life—you cannot trust this person in this season. And trust is a key component to sharing money and being in a relationship. Until trust is earned, you need to keep yourself safe, and that includes the money. I recommend counseling to determine if or when the money should be shared again.

Instead of spinning your wheels and letting your anger (and frustration) intensify without a solution, here's a framework to follow to evaluate if you need to keep your money SAFE:

Seek counseling if you experience
Abuse or addiction or
Financial infidelity, and
Evaluate your options and move forward with the help of a counselor

Danger Zone

When we feel anger, what we want at the core is for a wrong to be made right. In his book *The Voice of the Heart*, Chip Dodd describes anger as a deep want. In our bones we want justice, we want a solution, we want change, we want growth, or we want to be recognized.

In the case of money, it's the same thing. We want vindication from our debt, and we want validation. We want someone to say, "Yes, you got screwed. I see that. Here's your recompense." We want the apology!

Well, I can give you the validation for the anger, but unfortunately, a lot of us are allowing our anger to keep us sitting around waiting for someone else to pay for our debts, pay for our pain and suffering, and offer a heartfelt apology. The bad news is, that just ain't gonna happen. But the good news is, that anger boiling beneath the surface is exactly what you need. In fact, it's necessary for the justice you want to see with your money situation.

You *need* to feel that indignation rise up for you to want to actually *do* something. Your anger wants action. When it comes to anger, action is the antidote. But be careful, the wrong action can have the opposite effect—the wrong action can be poison.

In the Bible, there's a verse that includes, "In your anger do not sin" (Ephesians 4:26 NIV). Not *if you deal with anger.* No. It's expected that you will deal with anger in life. But the key is not to let anger—with money or with anything else—cause you to do the wrong things. Cussing out the Capitol One representative, for example, is not helpful. Allowing yourself to become bitter and envious of others who are winning with money is also not a good move.

But one of the most detrimental ways anger can influence us to do the wrong thing is by causing us to develop an "I deserve" mentality. "I deserve" can be a diabolical recipe for disaster for your money. And it can lead down a slippery slope of entitlement and envy. Here's how I saw it play out in my own life, and how I've seen it in the lives of the folks I coach.

Take It to the Limit

"I deserve to spend."

Remember late 2020 and early 2021? Americans were fed up with being cooped up inside for more than a year, social distancing, and sheltering in place due to the global COVID-19 pandemic. In retaliation, a new trend dubbed "revenge spending" took over.

Folks were going ham on trips and travel, Amazon boxes were showing up at doorsteps multiple times a day, and Lululemon was posting record sales revenue. The housing market turned into the Wild West (well, Southeast, really), as people loaded up their trucks and moved to "less expensive" locations, making reckless, sight-unseen offers on homes with tremendously inflated prices.

Meanwhile, those who stayed put took the boost in home equity as an opportunity to cash it all in on a new pool or to renovate their kitchen. Rash, foolish, impulsive behaviors. But we didn't care! Americans essentially said, "Screw this! I'm living my best life despite the financial repercussions. After all I've suffered with the pandemic, I deserve to treat myself. I deserve to do what I want to do."

It's spending to medicate our anger and emotional suffering. I've seen this play out in other ways too. I've listened over the phone lines as callers who've suffered all types of loss call in to confess their actions. Whether it's the passing of a loved one, a loss of employment, or the loss of a marriage, many of these folks have gone into inordinate amounts of credit card and other consumer debt as they wrestle with anger and other emotions of their loss. They may think, *After all that I went through, don't I deserve a break? Don't I deserve a reprieve?* And unfortunately, they find it (if only temporarily) in overspending.

Whether it's revenge spending or simply emotional spending, these are both frivolous behaviors that we engage in to curb anger and feel better. And they're rooted in the same mentality: I deserve.

On the flip side, financial success can also get us on that detrimental "I deserve" way of thinking. Like I mentioned earlier, during the last two years of our debt-free journey, our business was really taking off and we were earning more than we'd ever made—by far. Our income had eclipsed $200,000 a year, but you'd never know it because most of our margin was *still* going toward our debt. And as much of a blessing as it is to have a lot of margin to throw at debt, man, it kind of felt like taxes. Yes, it's great to make more money, but when you see that tax bill, it makes you want to shed a silent tear. So trust that sending a $6,000 payment to Navient didn't necessarily make me jump for joy.

I thought, *Man, I deserve to feel our success more than this! Shouldn't we spend some of this money?* Luckily, Sam and I had each other. So we each took turns talking the other off the "I deserve" ledge. But the truth is, that anger hits different when you can't have a lifestyle that you believe reflects your hard work and effort because of debt.

Those two little words are always whispering in our ear, hoping to steer us off track and appease our anger. But if we can recognize it for what it is—an emotional distraction—we can resist the temptation. We can go the opposite direction and double down on what we know to do because we know, in reality, each act of discipline is getting us to what we really want: financial peace, healing, and stability.

Speaking for Sam and me, the truth is, what we wanted *most* was not to spend more. Spending more simply represented recognition of all our hard work; it represented deserving a break. And while I wanted that, what I wanted *most* was to get to the debt-free life that we'd been working so hard to get to. I just wanted to be done. I wanted that accomplishment more than anything. Refocusing my anger to what I wanted most—justice for us when it came to money—was worth staying focused and disciplined.

EXAMINE YOUR ANGER

Take a moment to reflect on the "I deserve to spend" examples I shared above and think about some examples of how this has played out in your journey. Then take time to answer the questions below, so you can identify your *true* deep want.

Which "I deserve" thoughts can you see at work in your own life?

____

____

____

What does impulse or frivolous spending represent to you?

____

____

____

What is it you want now (the temptation)?

____

____

____

What is it you want most?

____

____

____

What would it look like to double down on doing what it takes to get what you want most?

____

____

____

It Should've Been Me

"I deserve what they have."

Call it jealousy. Call it being salty. Call it a passive-aggressive "must be nice" comment. Whatever you wanna call it, this offshoot of anger is not pretty. You know what I'm talking about. This is the "I deserve what they have" mentality that can develop when you're angry about what you don't have, and it comes out in this toxic comparison with someone who does have "it" (whatever "it" is). Or worse, it can cause you to get fixated on how it is that *they* deserve what they have. At this point, you're likely feeling envy creep in.

Here are a few behaviors that show what this deep-seated feeling of envy looks like:

- You have difficulty celebrating others.
- You're constantly comparing yourself to others (especially if you find yourself highlighting their privileges and ignoring your own blessings).
- You catch yourself making passive-aggressive "must be nice" comments:

  "Must be nice to have a spouse that pulls their own weight!"

  "If I had that income, I'd be out of debt too!"

  "All of us don't have the money for vacations like that."

  "They probably didn't even pay for it—her mother-in-law is probably helping them out."

Ooh-whee! I don't mean any harm, but like my mama used to say, you're too pretty to be acting that ugly! Trust me, I've been there. And it's not a good look. But more importantly, it's not getting us anywhere with our situation and our money.

The reality is, we each have our own race to run. Sure, we feel angry when we look up and feel like we're in last place! That's no fun. (Especially if you're competitive like I am.) But the thing is, we're not in some competition with other folks. We're just supposed to run our race to the best of our ability—we're trying to beat our personal best. The finish line is still the end point, regardless of when we cross.

So like it says in Proverbs, make sure that you're fixing your eyes straight ahead, giving careful thought to the paths of *your* feet and not turning to the right or left. This is a great reminder to stay focused on your actions and your race in front you.

Looking to the right at what Phil has in his retirement account at fifty-five, or to the left at Brenda's brand-new house, doesn't help you if all you're doing is comparing their race to yours. All that will do is get you all bent out of shape. If you're competing with Phil and Brenda but aren't on the same level playing field, you could feel like you're losing.

True competitions have considerations to make sure things start out fair. Life isn't like that. Because life's not a competition and life's not fair, the playing field is rarely level—everyone starts their financial race at different times and from different places. However, you can acknowledge where those folks are in their financial race so that you can "give careful thought to the paths for *your* feet."

I'd sum it up like this: Be curious, not critical. Be inquisitive, not competitive. What I'm saying is, you need to ask questions! Instead of scoffing and saying, "Must be nice . . . ," lean in and ask, "How did you do it?"

Here's what that looks like:

How did you find margin to save?
What side hustles worked best for you?
What type of work do you do? What degree is required for that line of work?
What was your process for saving your downpayment?
How did you build your income?
How did you land on that business idea?
Who did you work with to develop your business plan?
Do you use a professional to help you invest your money? Where did you find them?

Most people have no problem answering a few questions. And if they're *your* people, they were likely waiting for you to ask. They likely want to help! So be curious, not critical. Critical people compare and get annoyed or envious about other folks' wins. Curious people are interested in learning. Curious people are looking for the next right step they need to take.

EXAMINE YOUR ANGER

You know the drill here. Take a few minutes, grab a journal or use the space provided, and do some thinking about how this "I deserve what they have" mentality has played out for you. Be honest with yourself, and process however you need to so that you can aim to get to a place of curiosity.

Who in your life have you been competing with?

____

____

____

____

____

Who have you had a hard time celebrating?

____

____

____

Identify a few people who you could ask questions. Write their names down, then reach out.

____

____

____

This Is the Thanks I Get?!

"I don't deserve this."

The scenario started out perfectly. Sam and I found out we were pregnant just a few months before our tenth wedding anniversary, and we had an incredible celebration planned. Months earlier, we'd made the decision to push our Debt-Free Date by a few months so we could save up the cash to renew our vows on the exact same yacht we'd gotten married on. The idea of walking down the aisle surrounded by all our friends and family and saying yes to Sam all over again with our baby in my belly felt like a dream come true. By the time the baby would be born, we'd be completely debt-free. It felt like the perfect end to an amazing journey.

Sadly, it didn't go that way at all.

I don't think I've ever felt more angry or more cheated than I did sitting in that medical office as the doctor searched for the heartbeat. It wasn't there. I had miscarried our first child.

I waited over seven and a half years until the debt was gone to start a family, and this is the thanks I get? I had checked all my boxes. I had followed the steps. I had done my part. And yet, *this* is what I get? This must be some kind of sick joke. I remember thinking, *I don't deserve this . . . do I?*

I went home in disbelief. Crushed. Pissed. I was resentful of how things had gone down. I felt like I'd been taken for a ride. That child was the vision I'd seen that day on my run. That vision had kept me going all these years. And now it was just . . . gone? I wanted to yell out curses, kick up dust, and sob my eyes out. And I did.

I walked down the aisle at our vow renewal with tears in my eyes. But they were the wrong kind. Yes, of course, I was grateful for more years with my incredible husband. But I was angry and heartbroken about the loss we were both enduring. And in that moment, it somehow felt magnified.

Have you ever gone through a financial situation or a season so tough it leaves you asking the question, *Do I really deserve this?*

Whether it's a bankruptcy that took seven years to fall off your credit, an accident that left you disabled and unable to work at the career you'd trained for, a nasty divorce that took a decade to recover from, or being let go after you gave that company twenty years of your life—unfair things happen. And they make us angry. And we have a right to be. In our mind, this isn't how things were supposed to be. We want to shake our fist at the clouds above. We want to rant and scream and weep. And in my humble opinion, we should.

"I will give free rein to my complaint and speak out in the bitterness of my soul" (Job 10:1 NIV). This came directly from a guy in the Bible named Job. He was a good man who lost *everything*. He was a good man who got a raw deal. He had a lot to be upset about. And so, he was—and he didn't try to hide it. Holding it in does no good. Letting it out is therapeutic. But what next?

What I'm about to tell you next is something that I can confirm is true from the other side of anger and disappointment. But truthfully, in the moment of my anger and pain—I just had to have faith in it.

Here it is: **Nothing is wasted. I promise.**

Have you ever had a moment that triggers a deep memory that you didn't even know was in you? Well, when I was in the depths of my anger over working so hard to right our financial wrongs and only being met with loss, a random saying came to my mind that I didn't even know was in me. I googled it just to be sure. And sure enough, it was a promise from the Bible: "I will give you back what you lost to the swarming locusts, the hopping locusts, the stripping locusts, and the cutting locusts. . . . And you will praise the Lord your God, who does these miracles for you. Never again will my people be disgraced" (Joel 2:25–26 NLT).

For clarity, back in the day, locusts were a big problem. They completely consumed crops and harvests, causing catastrophic economic losses. For me, it felt like years of my life had been "eaten up" with the consequences of our debt. And then I felt disgraced after losing my baby. It felt like so much time had been consumed and utterly wasted. And I was mad about it. But now I can see that nothing was wasted. These days it's clear as day, and I wouldn't trade our journey for the world. God didn't cause those challenges, but He trusted me with them, and He used them to make me who I am. Turns out, I could trust Him too—He has used every last drop of our pain and anger. None of it was wasted. And because of that, this promise has become a cornerstone of Sam's and my story.

In many ways, it feels like we've been given back the time we lost with our money journey because we've been able to grow so fast now that we're out of debt. I believe the same can be true for you. What was intended for harm, what caused great pain or suffering, can be used for your good. But you can't quit. You have to keep moving forward, doing what you know to do.

ADJUST YOUR ANGER

I'll go ahead and say, doing that is not always easy. But to get the ball rolling, I want you to work through these questions. Just like before, feel free to use the pages in this book or use these questions as prompts in your own journal.

What is the raw deal you have faced as it relates to your money?

____

____

____

____

What feels unfair?

___

___

___

The next few lines are for you to "speak out in the bitterness of your soul." Don't hold back!

___

___

___

Now say this out loud: **Nothing is wasted.** That's the mantra that you must repeat again and again as you continue forward.

___

___

___

We Are the Champions

Now, I've always been a competitive person with an intense personality. Of course, I like to win. But even more than that, I *hate* the feeling of losing. Back in my basketball and college volleyball days, if my team was down or playing poorly, I'd start to feel anger rising up. Early on, I had to learn how to refocus my anger into action on the court. That anger created a fire of motivation inside of me that acted like fuel—fuel to go beyond my emotions and get the job done, whether it was the first of many games in a championship series or the final match-up with just seconds on the clock.

That counterattack of turning anger into action that served me so well in sports is what I needed to tap into for finishing the job with our debt. Then Sam and I took that same intensity into going on the offensive to finally build our way through Baby Steps 3, 4, and beyond. But what is actually happening here? You'll know when your anger is in the right place when it's strongly attached to a meaningful motivation. I described it earlier when I told you about refocusing my anger against debt and credit scores. I wanted to beat the credit cards at their own game and win back my financial peace. So it's not just you ranting and raving and yelling at the refs. This is about locking in and making your response produce actual change.

That's the positive side of anger: when it seeks to produce real, needed growth and change. As a matter of fact, in many situations where I've been angry, I've found it can be more helpful to say "I'm motivated" instead of "I'm angry." When we do this, we're keeping the focus on doing something meaningful. Even if the meaningful thing is to grieve in a healthy way and not give up hope.

Don't just get mad, get motivated.

- In the face of a spouse who is wearing you out with their impulse spending: "I'm motivated for us to find a solution to this overspending."

- In response to an unforeseen loss: "I'm motivated to find the silver lining."
- In response to the reality of where you are financially: "I'm extremely motivated to get our emergency fund stacked up."

Anger won't get you far by itself. But when channeled through meaningful motivation, it can work wonders.

Fire

Man, this was deep. I feel like we know each other on a whole other level now! But that's what happens when we start talking about the emotional side of money. And it turns out, anger is really one to dig into. I want to leave you with one final way to think of anger.

Anger is like fire.

Fire is powerful. If you're reckless in your anger, and allow it to make you hostile or retaliatory, it will destroy everything you're trying to build. But if you wield it the right way, with meaningful motivation, it can blaze the path to where you want to go, and it can be the flame under your butt to keep you moving.

Fire, like any energy source, requires fuel. So the question is, what's fueling your fire? Is it that toxic "I deserve" air? Or are you fueling your fire with good, clean air by doubling down on what you know to do, running your own race, asking the right questions to get ahead, and deciding that, no matter what, nothing is wasted?

MOTIVATE YOUR ANGER

What you do with your fire is up to you. So go ahead and take a moment to decide. Answer these questions to discover your next steps forward.

How will you let the "royal scam" fuel your fire in a good way? What's your meaningful motivation?

____

____

____

Since action is the antidote to anger, what is the right next step to put your new meaningful motivation into action?

____

____

____

Mercy Me

I wanna take a moment to give you the last 2 percent. A lot of times when we have conversations, there's a last little bit we leave out for varying reasons, many of which are fear-based. I don't operate like that anymore. So I'm gonna shoot you straight. When we feel mad because the bills are stacking up and our money is not where we think it should be, or because we feel like we got scammed by the credit game or all the other things we've talked about, it's really easy for our anger to cloud our perspective. And those "I deserve" thoughts—and the behaviors that come from them—can run rampant. Look, I get it. I do.

But if I'm gonna tell you the full, honest, real truth, it's this: We don't deserve jack.

"Deserve" is a trap. And whenever I feel myself going down that road, especially when it's anger steering me, I have to remind myself that I deserve nothing.

The Bible says every good and perfect gift comes down from above! My pastor used to say: If you got it and it's good, it's from God. Meaning, if my income increases—even if I don't get to use it in all the ways I wish I could—it's still a blessing; it's still a gift from God. It's God showing His grace toward me. It's not about what I deserve. Because let's be real, remember the way I handled money before? Shoot! It was only by the mercy of God that I was given the opportunity and the mindset shift to want to get it right.

I heard someone explain God's grace and mercy like this: Grace is when we get what we don't deserve. Mercy is when we don't get what we do deserve.

I don't deserve the blessings I have today. And for that, I'm thankful. I didn't suffer the full consequences that could've taken place because of my mistakes. It could've been so much worse. And for that, I'm thankful.

My truth is, when you start to filter your financial anger through the truth of grace and mercy, anger starts to take a backseat and a bigger emotion starts pushing through: thankfulness.

EMBRACE THANKFULNESS

So take a moment and shift your focus. Use the questions below as an opportunity to find the silver lining in your anger.

What are you thankful for amid your anger?

____

____

____

What's an example of grace you can identify in your situation?

____

____

____

What's an example of mercy you've witnessed in the midst of your money mistakes?

____

____

____

CHAPTER NINE

SELF-PITY

Oh, Good Grief

My mother-in-law, whom we all call "Bubbie" (Yiddish for "Grandma"), is one of the most generous humans I've ever met when it comes to her family. Bubbie has always been there for us when we needed her, especially when Sam and I were struggling to get out of debt and get a hold of our finances. Bubbie gave us more financial gifts of her own volition than I can list.

It was her townhouse that we rented at cost for more than eight years. She regularly took us out for dinners and lunches when paying for a meal at a restaurant was the last thing we could afford. Not to mention, each year we woke up at the butt crack of dawn the day after Thanksgiving and Bubbie took us Black Friday shopping. She'd spend hundreds of dollars on clothes and shoes and everything we could possibly need. When the time finally came for us to buy a house, it was Bubbie who gifted us money to help with a down payment and help renovate our kitchen. And when we were expecting, it was Bubbie who bought the crib and furniture for both our children. She truly spoiled us.

One of her signature moves was, and still is, sending us celebratory cards. Every birthday, anniversary, and holiday, we can count on a greeting card from Bubbie, complete with a sweet message and at least $100 cash inside. And let me tell you something: Back in the day, that cash in those cards always came in clutch. Now while Bubbie likely intended for the money to be spent on doing something fun or buying ourselves something special, from 2008 to 2016, that money went to bills.

And a lot of times, it was there just in time to bail us out of a jam. I remember putting the money toward paying our cell phone bill one year. Another time, it went toward getting current on our credit card payments. And one Valentine's Day, instead of the money going to a romantic date night with Sam, I remember the distinctly unromantic feeling of us deciding to use the money toward getting our overdrawn bank account out of the red and back (ever so slightly) into the black.

I think I speak for Sam too, when I say I never felt more sorry for myself than I did in those moments. I'd think to myself, *Man, this sucks! I don't even get to keep this gift I'm meant to enjoy.*

Back then, it felt like no matter what, we just couldn't catch a break. If our financial life was a cartoon character, we'd be Charlie Brown.

> Lucy: "Charlie Brown, you blockhead! You used my Valentine's card to pay your utilities. I can't believe it! What kind of person uses a gift like that to pay their bills?"

Charlie Brown: "Oh, brother. Well, I at least *thought* about using it for fun. They say it's the thought that counts."

What a sad state of affairs. It was those moments of sacrifice that made me realize the gravity of our financial situation. The truth is, in those moments, I felt sorry for myself. *Woe is me!* And in those moments, I'll admit, there were little moments of hopelessness. Like I wanted to just give up. Why even try?

As silly as it sounds, those times of not being able to enjoy a simple gift . . . it felt like we were being kicked while we were already down. Poor, pitiful Jade. Poor, pitiful Sam. And there it is, self-pity rearing its ugly head.

Self-Pity: *A feeling of self-absorbed unhappiness over one's own troubles.*

Self-pity creates a toxic cynicism inside of us. And if we aren't careful, pity will eat away at our hope until we eventually give up. That's why it's so important to catch it and get your mind right.

The truth is, there are legit things that you will miss out on in the name of saving money while you're working to get out of debt or hit a goal. It's a bummer when you can't go out to dinner with the girls or afford the couples' trip. And it's easy to feel sorry for yourself. In our situation, spending that celebration cash on keeping the ball rolling was the right move. And although I felt self-pity in the moment, I also know I never let it win or get the best of me. Because here's the thing: When you let pity stick around too long, self-pity will convince you to turn a good reason into a bad excuse.

Here's what I mean. Considering the state of our finances, Sam and I had good reason to feel down in the dumps. There were plenty of reasons to say, "I *do* deserve to spend this money on a good time! Look at how hard we've been working." Heck, we had all the reasons in the world to just throw up our hands and say, "This is too much. Plenty of people live with debt—we'll just be one of them." But that would be letting self-pity get the best of us. The moment you let those reasons stop you from doing the things you know you need to do, the moment you let them stop you from taking the next right step forward, is the moment they become excuses.

You see, self-pity and anger are connected. In chapter 8, I talked about how anger is a flame. When you feed it the right fuel, it can push you forward. Self-pity takes over when the flame of anger goes out and you just become . . . a victim.

And victims make a lot of excuses.

But the good news is, you *can* get yourself out of self-pity, even if you're already in victim mode, and I'll show you how. But first, we'll look at how to recognize self-pity—what it looks, sounds, and feels like in our daily life—so you can catch it before it takes over.

Cry Me a River

Adult Advisory: I'm about to tell you the truth, the whole truth, and nothing but the truth about self-pity in this chapter. Some of it might be hard to accept. But we've gotten this far together, so I won't hold back on you now. This is going to help you, I promise—but still, gird your loins.

What Self-Pity Feels Like

First, let me just say that feeling some small amount of self-pity is common when it comes to money. It can start to rise up when you're disappointed with your current situation and the apparent lack of impact your actions are having in combating what's "*been done to you.*" (I emphasize what's *been done to you* because pity tends to feel like a victim mentality.)

A major symptom of self-pity is when you find yourself thinking or saying things like, *[Outside factors x, y, z] are holding me back, and I can't control them because they're external.*

Some of those outside factors might come in the form of things like:

- Predatory student loan programs
- The election cycle
- Inflation
- High interest rates
- The housing market
- COVID-19
- The school you attended
- The neighborhood where you grew up
- The job market
- Your parents

- Your ex
- Your boss
- The president

Now, these are all extremely valid factors that can shape our experience and decisions with money. But a person who's caught in self-pity feels like they're a victim of these factors. They're a victim of the system. Remember our car illustration? If behavior is a car, belief is in the driver's seat and emotion steers the wheel. If you truly believe you're a victim and there is nothing you can do to change your situation, you won't press on the gas. And regardless of where pity steers the wheel, you'll remain stuck.

Have you heard of Katherine Johnson? If you haven't, I highly recommend watching the movie *Hidden Figures*. It's based on the true story of Johnson, a black female mathematician who worked for NASA for thirty-three years. She was a key contributor to countless projects, including the historic 1969 Apollo 11 moon-landing mission. She's also credited as one of the first African American NASA scientists.

The movie specifically follows Johnson's work on the Friendship 7 Mission in 1962, when John Glenn completed the first American orbit around Earth. Johnson helped calculate trajectories, launch windows, and return paths to make the orbit a success.

Now, you wanna talk about external factors that could hold someone back? Here are a few that Katherine Johnson had to overcome: First off, workplace segregation laws. Johnson was entirely separated from her white (mostly male) colleagues. She and her African American colleagues were forced to utilize a bathroom, cafeteria, and workspace across the campus. One article stated that their workspace was literally labeled "colored computers." And being physically separated also meant Johnson was separated from what was taking place in real time with their work. Being left out of important meetings that affected the math made it difficult for her to use her time efficiently. Not to mention, as a black female in a white male-dominated space, she had to speak up adamantly to be included, work harder to be seen, and fight harder for a seat at the table. In an ecosystem designed to make her feel out of place and less than, Johnson didn't have the luxury of making mistakes or excuses.

Just listing this out sounds like a lot of stress, a lot of external forces pushing against her, a lot of opportunities to fail, and a lot of justification to quit. There were plenty of reasons to have a pity party and give up! Instead, she excelled. How she soldiered forward in the face of that level of aggression is astounding and inspiring. But it wasn't just her skill as a mathematician that caused her success. It was her mindset and perspective.

When asked about life working for NASA in those days, Johnson once said, "I didn't feel the segregation at NASA because everybody there was doing research. You had a mission, and you worked on it, and it was important to you to do your job. . . . I didn't feel any segregation. I knew it was there, but I didn't feel it."[20]

Those are the words of a person who knows what to focus on. Those are the words of a person very much in control of their emotions. Those are the words of a person not interested in "excuses," no matter how valid. Those are the words of a person who knows how to block out the real disadvantages and prejudices that exist in order to get things done.

So if you believe that you have no control over how external factors and adversity affect you, it's likely time to change how you feel about adversity.

I'd challenge you to start viewing adversity as an opportunity. I've learned over the years that adversity is actually an invitation to be great. Accomplishing something against all odds is what we cheer for in life. Think about it! All the greats have struggled to overcome external factors stacked against them. Michael Jordan didn't make his JV basketball team. Franklin D. Roosevelt was paralyzed from the waist down due to polio. Millionaire and *Shark Tank* angel investor Robert Herjavec was the first-generation American son of Croatian immigrants who came to America with only $20. Venus and Serena Williams had to navigate low income and the streets of Compton. They all overcame circumstances and obstacles and never gave up.

Want a more everyday example? Go to *The Ramsey Show* YouTube channel and watch some of the many Debt-Free Screams from over the years. These aren't celebrities or sports legends. These are everyday people who won with their money. And you'll see the same theme in every story: The adversity they faced didn't diminish their belief that they could do great things—it strengthened it. Perhaps it's time for you to view adversity as an opportunity to step up, not step back. External financial adversity is a valid reason for why things may be tough, but it's not an excuse to give up.

When I first heard Johnson's story, I loved it. It reminded me of how I was raised. My parents didn't teach us kids to focus on the disparities or disadvantages or lack of privileges we might face because we might not be able to control those. My dad simply told us that we are to walk into the room as leaders. He taught us to see ourselves as leaders—and to work and behave as the leaders we are. My dad pushed us to focus on small winning habits we could do daily. Habits we could control, like making our beds every morning, being on time, working hard, and always "tuck your shirt tail in" (his way of saying to always look your best). As a result, instead of focusing on the noise, I focused on who I was and my habits of the day.

The same thing applies with money. Amid all the external forces—the inequalities, the gaps, the administrations, the frustrations, and the unfairness of it all—if you step into your finances and focus on what you control, you can begin to win. Stop and remind yourself, "I'm the leader here; I'm in control." Because no matter what is going on in Washington, DC, you are the leader of your household, and you are the one deciding what you do with your money. Push yourself to focus on your daily money habits, like checking in with your budget before you spend and tracking your transactions.

But whatever habits you embrace and whatever you do, don't let those good reasons become bad excuses. Don't let self-pity keep you from taking the next right step. The cards may be stacked against you—you may have come from a low-income upbringing or had a recent job loss or had a friend or business partner steal from you—but you get to choose where you direct your focus.

Whatever It Takes

What Self-Pity Sounds Like

Self-pity starts on the inside, but the effects of it quickly make their way out. All the negativity we've been ruminating on and all our beliefs about why our situation is pitiful start to come out of our mouth. There's a proverb that says out of the abundance of your heart, your mouth speaks. Meaning that any beliefs that live inside you, you will begin to say out loud. And it sounds a lot like a pity party: "Because of [x, y, z], I'm nowhere close to where I should be with my money—and since [x, y, z], there's no way for someone like me to get there."

When it comes down to it, self-pity sounds like someone who'd rather be right than happy. I hear it all the time hosting *The Ramsey Show.* This is the person who would rather be right that all the injustices, inconveniences, and lack of privileges they've experienced mean they're stuck for good, than be happy and hopeful about the fact that there is a solution for each of us.

I distinctly remember one lady who called into *The Ramsey Show*. She was a stay-at-home mom with school-aged children, but the house was too expensive, and she and her husband were feeling the struggle of her not having an income. From the beginning of the call, I sensed that she didn't really want my advice. She wanted to complain—and wanted me to agree with her that there was no way out. Instead, I offered option after option as a path forward: She could work part-time outside the house or find a work-from-home role, they could downsize, they could pay off the car to find margin. One by one, she shot down each option with a reason why it wouldn't work. Finally, I stopped her.

"Look, it doesn't matter what I say," I told her. "You don't want a solution—you want to be right. You want me to validate your pity party!"

She was content to let her reasons be excuses not to embrace uncomfortable solutions. Choosing hope and choosing to pursue a solution wasn't something I could do for her. A person has to be willing to choose hope in their own situation—and there are plenty of stories out there of people who do choose hope and choose a path forward, even when neither seems to exist. Take Sydney Polak for example.

Sydney Polak was one of nine siblings—six boys and three girls. When he was young, his entire family was captured in Poland in the midst of the Holocaust because of their Jewish descent. During World War II, more than six million Jews were killed, and sadly, Sydney's family was no exception. He witnessed virtually his entire family get murdered right in front of him. Sydney, his father, and his brother Louie were the only ones kept alive. Sydney and Louie were sent to separate work camps—he in Russia and his brother in Siberia. His father was sent to Auschwitz, where he later died.

Somehow, Sydney managed to escape and join the Italian Army until the end of the war. In 1948, he made it over the ocean to New York. Even though he didn't speak English, Sydney was still able to get a job as a cook. Later, he worked on the Empire State Building and learned the trade of a glass glazer. From there, he started several businesses, including a home improvement business and later an artwork framing business. Eventually, he moved down to south Florida and opened an art shop in Hollywood, which he named after his daughter—who happens to be my mother-in-law, our Bubbie.

Sydney, who Sam always called "Zadie" (Yiddish for "Grandfather"), passed away while Sam and I were engaged, before I got the chance to meet him. While I never met him, I know his legacy. Zadie died a multimillionaire. Despite the horrific experiences and unimaginable tragedies he'd gone through, this man found the will to take the next right step again and again. The only thing that could give a person that kind of strength is hope. And in the process, he left an inheritance to his children's children, his wife, and extended family.

The monetary inheritance Sam received went directly toward student loans, of course. But in learning Zadie's story, I indirectly received a legacy of hard work, perseverance, entrepreneurship, and the belief that good reasons never have to be excuses to give up. Hope abides. And that legacy went directly toward adjusting my own mentality and actions surrounding our life and our money.

I remember that when Sam told me all about what Zadie had endured, I thought, *Man, what a story. What grit.* Suddenly, I looked at the adversity that Sam and I were facing with a new perspective. If there was ever a person who had reason to give up, it was Zadie. But he never did.

If he can do that, we can surely do this, I thought.

Now don't get me wrong—struggles are relative. My goal is not to diminish anyone's struggles through comparison. But when we hear other people's stories, it can give us a new perspective to look at our own stories. And sometimes, a little perspective is just what we need to shake ourselves out of self-pity.

Sometimes we have to look at how bad others got it to see how good we got it. Again, I'm not talking about getting into a habit of comparison—I'm simply talking about developing a new perspective. Sometimes we've gotta admit that we're not where we want to be, but it's better than where we used to be and better than where we could be. For me, hearing a story like Zadie's was all I needed to gain a little wind in my sails. Hopefully, you can gain a little inspiration and perspective from his story as well.

Author and business coach Tony Robbins once said, "Whatever you look for, you'll find." It's especially true when we're facing a pitiful situation with our money. If you choose to look for reasons to remain stuck and reasons why it's impossible to get ahead, you will most definitely find them. But if you choose to look for reasons why it is possible to win and to look for ways to win, no matter the situation, you will most definitely find those as well. And when you find them, grab on to them with all your might. Because self-pity wants you to believe that your situation is hopeless—but it's not. We have to make the conscious decision to look for hope. Hope is something you have to choose.

Thank You, Next

What Self-Pity Looks Like

Nothing creates the perfect environment for self-pity to thrive like social media. If you're battling a pity party, my advice is to handle social media with great caution and great care. Or honestly, just avoid it altogether. Otherwise, next thing you know, you'll be doomscrolling posts about why it's impossible to be a millionaire in America today. Or worse, you'll be blowing up other folks' DMs, slamming them for a post they made on how they accomplished their financial success.

Financial self-pity looks like someone who's been coddled and has a sense of financial entitlement. They define the discomfort, struggle, or challenge to obtain their financial goals as some sort of personal injustice. This is the hallmark of self-pity I see playing out all over social media. It can look like trolling other people's positive money posts and making negative comments to make yourself feel better. Or it can also show up in what I call "coddle culture," which looks like this:

- An Instagram post that says, "Anyone who would tell you not to go to restaurants while getting out of debt is a *toxic* influence."
- An X post that says, "This narrative that we can just pull ourselves up and out of debt in the midst of this economy is just *gaslighting* the realities of record inflation."
- A Facebook post that says, "Cutting out the things that give you joy, and putting yourself through financial

> *trauma*, is not a healthy way to pay off debt. You shouldn't have to sacrifice your joy to enjoy your money."

Oh, give me a break! What a crock of total BS. Respectfully, these folks are choosing to have a pity party. *Woe is me! Reality is unfair! These big, bad experts want me to actually work and do hard things! The nerve!* When you see posts like these, it's best to say, "Thank you, next!" and keep scrolling.

Now, don't get me wrong. I don't have an issue with words like *toxic*, *trauma*, and *gaslighting* when they're used in the right scenario and in the right context. But it's not a stretch to say that these words are *way* overused, especially in social media. There's a time and place for these words, but this is not it. If you hear yourself using this kind of language to get a pass from putting in the work to get what you want out of life, you're only "gaslighting" yourself. You're trying to convince yourself that reality isn't true.

The reality is, hard work is . . . hard.

The reality is, anything worth having is worth the sacrifice to get it.

The reality is, the struggle is not only real; it's also *necessary* for us to become our best selves. I'd argue that someone who wishes to avoid struggle is just, well, immature.

The truth is, we should view struggles as opportunities to grow—just like it says in the book of James: "When troubles of any kind come your way, consider it an opportunity for great joy. For you know that when your faith is tested, your endurance has a chance to grow" (1:2–3 NLT). The passage goes on to say that we should let endurance grow because when endurance is fully developed, it causes us to be "perfect and complete, needing nothing" (verse 4).

So if you want to be mature with your money, you've gotta embrace the things that require endurance. The hard things. By now, I'm sure it's clear that getting on a plan for your money and walking the Baby Steps will require endurance. The good news is that it will result in money maturity.

Simply put, money maturity means you can consider yourself a financially responsible adult. You've become fully developed. You're regularly walking the Baby Steps; therefore, you're now a person who lives on a budget, you're a person who actively says no to debt, you understand the importance of saving for the future, and you prioritize generosity. You're sticking it out in the hard things, and you've started to develop maturity.

Coddle culture and avoiding hard things won't get you there. The truth is, there is great reward in putting yourself to the test. To beat pity, you must choose endurance, not avoidance. Challenging yourself to stick to a budget is not toxic. Doing the hard work of paying off debt is not traumatic. Being willing to take control of your money in any economy isn't gaslighting. So for anyone interested in moving beyond self-pity, it's time to ditch the coddle culture, stop trolling, and get our hands dirty doing the work. And doing the work starts with saying yes.

I know, it's an earth-shattering idea. But saying yes is like signing on the dotted line. It's a commitment to try a new idea or process that is proven to get you where you want to go . . . even if there's a little discomfort or a little struggle that goes with it. And the good news is not only that you will accomplish your goal; you'll also build the muscle of endurance and be able to show off some massive maturity gains.

Photograph

I'll never forget the Christmas of 2012. Sam and I were still neck deep in our debt and still extremely far away from the finish line. Despite our woes, it was the holiday season. But it seemed like that gay, happy feeling was in the air for everyone but us. Paying our way through $460,000 of debt meant that this Christmas was *not* the year to spend extra money on things like . . . well, Christmas.

Don't get me wrong. I wasn't out there trying to be a buzzkill. Sam and I just knew this was not a year to do the most if we ever wanted to accomplish our debt-free dream. Instead, we decided to focus on working as much possible and spending as little as possible. But all the while, we were both struggling to keep ourselves from falling into a pit of pity. So I did all I could. I remember standing in the middle of our townhome with my hands on my hips, looking around the place thinking, *What can I do to get our spirits up?*

I had a miniature tabletop Christmas tree that I'd bought at Big Lots for less than ten bucks. I found a random strand of lights in the garage and wrapped them around the banister. I knew we couldn't afford a big Christmas dinner, so I picked the furthest, cheapest meal from it: baked potato soup. Sam and I decided not to exchange gifts that year, but I made a pan of homemade cinnamon rolls as a special treat.

I was feeling pretty good about our little Charlie Brown Christmas, and then it happened: I got knocked swiftly out of my own contentment and into the pity pit by, shocker, social media. Instagram was relatively new, and back then, it was really just a place for bad food pics, duckface selfies, and peoples' highlight reels. And I knew this! But when I opened that app on Christmas morning, it was enough to take me out of being okay with our quaint Christmas to being full of self-pity. I saw big, beautifully decorated trees lined with presents. Perfect family photos with everyone in matching pajamas. Trips to Disney. Incredible holiday meal spreads. Gifts people had received and posted with the caption "#blessed."

No shade, but these kinds of posts are self-absorbed, and they cause others to get self-absorbed too. As a matter of fact, we get so absorbed in our own selves and all that we *don't* have and *aren't* accomplishing, that we start to spiral into pity-party mode. The truth is, I wanted to cry. I felt sorry for myself. I felt pitiful. And I know Sam did too. In that moment, I saw everything we didn't have, and it felt so unfair.

Now earlier in this chapter, we talked about comparing stories to help find inspiration or to learn, but what I'm talking about is the negative kind of comparison. This kind of comparison is only a distraction that makes you feel bad about yourself. And if there were ever two people with the right to get onboard with the ideas of coddle culture I listed before, it should've been us! But in that moment, there was one thing that helped Sam and me through it.

Every year we do a tradition called Greatest Gift. Sam and I decide on an amount that we want to give, and then we give it on Christmas Day. That year was no different. What I learned is the ultimate way to get out of self-pity is to get out of self. And the way to get out of self is to think about others. In this way, generosity is the ultimate antidote to self-pity. It causes you to get out of your selfish thinking and pouting and put the focus on blessing others rather than comparing yourself with them. And here's the secret: You can't be a pity and a blessing at the same time.

If money is just too tight, remember that there are a lot of ways we can be generous. We can give our talents, our words, and our time—the latter of which is often a big need. There are always opportunities to give time to community organizations or local churches.

When Sam and I were getting out of debt, we gave our time by helping others on the same journey by teaching Financial Peace University. It was a great way to get out of self-centered self-pity by remembering we were not all by ourselves.

You're not alone either. Self-pity can make us feel isolated, like we're the only one who's broke and struggling to make ends meet. But finding ways to give reminds us that we aren't the only ones fighting the good fight.

The Show Must Go On

If I had to wrap self-pity up with a neat little bow, I'd say it's more than just a feeling of self-absorbed unhappiness over one's own troubles or a belief that one has suffered a lot of injustices—or even a quiet hopelessness. Self-pity has a darker side. We can now see that it's also a self-absorbed, self-destructive, "rather be right than happy," "I'm the victim" emotional state that keeps a lot of folks cynical, unmotivated, unsatisfied, and stuck with their money. Okay, that's a big bow, but it's true.

Thankfully, we don't have to stay there. There are a lot of good reasons why getting your money on track may be difficult. But you can't allow self-pity to take over and turn those good reasons into bad excuses to give up. You've come too far!

Below you'll find action items and writing prompts to keep you going when you're facing adversity. Take some time to work through each item on the checklist before moving to the next chapter—and be sure to bookmark this page for you to revisit anytime you need an extra boost.

PLOW THROUGH SELF-PITY

✔ **Look at adversity as an opportunity to step up, not step back.**

Take Note: What are you facing that may be causing some self-pity to bubble up? List those things out. Now brainstorm a few ways you can step up in the midst of these situations.

Take Action: Make a plan to put those "ways to step up" that you listed into action.

✔ **Keep doing the things you know to do.**

Take Note: There are plenty of things you can't control, but there are also things you *can* control. List three things out of your control that are directly affecting your money goals in an adverse way. Then list three things within your control that can directly affect your money goals in a positive way.

Take Action: Implement these three Daily Money Habits: (1) Check your budget before spending. (2) Track your transactions. (3) Remind yourself that you're in control.

✔ **Be intentional about looking for reasons to hope.**

Take Action: Go on YouTube and watch a few Debt-Free Scream videos from *The Ramsey Show.*

Take Note: How did the stories accompanying the Debt-Free Screams make you feel?

✔ **Find inspiration in the stories of others (like you're doing in this book!).**

Take Note: There's something about writing things down on paper that makes them more real. Write an inspirational story about your money journey with you as the main character. Write about what you "overcame," how you did it, and where you are "now" as a result of your hard work and dedication.

Take Action: Finish reading this book and go put the teachings into action!

✔ **Ditch coddle culture and choose endurance, not avoidance.**

Take Note: Think back on the past few years. When has social media skewed your ideas of what's possible with money? How has it influenced your perspective on what it takes to get ahead?

Take Action: Do a social media cleanse. Consider taking a thirty-day break from social media or unfollowing any accounts that don't lift you up and show you hope.

✔ **Get out of self and get generous.**

Take Note: How can you embrace generosity in your life, starting right away? Write down three ideas for how you can be generous with your time, and three ideas for how you can be generous with your money.

Take Action: Pick one specific way to give your time and one specific way to give your money, and do those in the next month. (Make sure to learn about the cause you'd be supporting so you feel connected to your generosity.)

If you can get good at shutting self-pity down, you're well on your way to the next emotion along this crazy journey. And good news! This next emotion is an indicator that you've hit a crucial turning point. It means you're gonna make it because you've finally come to a point of acceptance.

I can't wait to show you how reaching acceptance will allow you to drive the rest of the way to your financial dreams.

CHAPTER TEN

ACCEPTANCE

Vertigo

Several years back, Sam and I had the opportunity to help two of our best friends, Porshia and Quency, with their money. It all started when we invited them to join our Financial Peace University class. Once a week, our class members got together to work on our money and learn how to walk the Baby Steps, but Quency and Porshia were extra inquisitive. At the time, they were engaged, and Porshia, the daughter of Haitian immigrants, and Quency, the son of Panamanian immigrants, each had a vested interest in taking control of their financial destiny. For them, this was an opportunity to change their family tree.

Week after week, we sat with them after hours to work on their individual budgets, talk through how they could each make progress on their own debt, and discuss what it would look like for them to combine their money once they were married. They were in their early twenties and were still solidifying their entertainment careers. So Sam and I were able to encourage them to work as much as possible and show them what it could look like to start a business of their own.

After several weeks of giving them a deep dive on the Baby Steps, I started to notice something. Every time we met, they asked question after question—which is totally normal—but I started to notice that these were the same questions they'd asked many times before.

"Do we take *all* the savings and put it on the debt?"

"Girl, I just finished paying off my car. I gotta keep going with the same intensity?"

"Do I need to include Cash App money in the budget?"

I knew *they* knew the answer. The problem was, they weren't fully ready to take action. They'd worked through a lot of emotion at this point, but they hadn't reached the acceptance phase yet. And if you've made it this far into this book, you're likely in a similar spot—or at least, you're well on your way. So what is acceptance?

Acceptance: *a willingness to tolerate difficult or unpleasant circumstances to get to the outcome you want.*

Basically, this is where you are when you've made peace with the process. And it's important to call out that acceptance is a little different than our other emotions. Because it's not *just* an emotion. It's actually more of a state of mind. Emotions tend to be in a moment and transient (which is why it's so problematic to get stuck in them). A state of mind, however, is more of an ongoing way of thinking and interpreting things, which is exactly what you need.

Acceptance isn't an emotion you need to move on from. It's a state of mind I want you to exist in. Once you reach acceptance, you can recognize that all these emotions you've been feeling are real and valid, but they don't have to last forever—and you don't have to let them stop you. You can move forward in the midst of them.

Acceptance is key because it leads to ownership of your actions from here on out. Getting to acceptance will help you stay on pace and run the race despite all the emotional reasons not to—the frustration, fear, anger, guilt, shame, and pity. Acceptance also leads to responsibility. You accept the fact that no matter what you may feel, and no matter if your financial struggles and barriers are entirely your fault or not, *you* are the one responsible for your life. *You* are the only one who can push Play and move forward.

What happens next depends on one person and one person alone, and that's you.

Squabble Up

So going back to our friends Porshia and Quency, this was the last turn they needed to truly start making progress. They were doing the FPU class. They were asking the questions. What were they missing?

Well, those relentless questions, as it turns out, told me exactly what was going on: Their emotions were getting the best of them.

The reality of what it was going to take out of each of them was setting in, and they were having a hard time accepting it.

In his book *Atomic Habits*, James Clear describes this as motion versus action.[21] Motion is when someone just keeps chasing more information and knowledge but doesn't make a real move. Action is actually doing the thing. Action comes when you begin to put all the information to work. Motion *feels* productive, but action is what gets results.

I call this stage of obsessive information gathering something different. I call it "being an ask hole." This is someone who asks the same question, or variations of the same questions, over and over but doesn't actually use the information. With the Baby Steps, it happens all the time. I can't tell you how many folks call into *The Ramsey Show* and say, "I've been a listener for ten years!" and then explain that they think they are ready to get out of debt but aren't sure where to get started. *Sigh.* Years of getting, getting, getting but no doing.

Luckily for Quency and Porshia, it didn't take years. It only took a few months. At one point, they came to the house, and as they started jumping in with the same old questions, I finally stopped them. I looked at them and said something to the effect of, "Hey, you know the answer to this already. It's going to be uncomfortable, you will have to sacrifice, and it will take a while. You're either going to do it or you're not."

Something must've clicked that day. Because from then on, it was "challenge accepted." Sam and I started seeing more progress than we'd ever seen from those two. They started killing it! They worked around the clock, budgeted every dollar, temporarily cut out unnecessary spending, and worked together toward their goals. They accepted what it would take to win, and they did the plan to make it happen. The next year was 2020—the pandemic year—and despite all the external factors and fatigue, they continued going at light speed.

Finally, on Christmas Eve of 2021, Porshia and Quency came over to our house, and at the island in our kitchen, they opened the laptop and hit Send on their final payment. Y'all, I shouted! I was so happy for them that I cried ice-cold tears of joy. I knew firsthand the impact their decision would have on their individual lives, marriage, and future family.

These first-generation Americans, a newly married vocalist and dancer in their late twenties, paid off over $75,000—in the midst of a pandemic that directly affected their jobs—because they accepted what it would take to cross the finish line and they fully committed. Challenge accepted. Family tree forever changed.

You can tell me you won't do it, but please don't tell me you can't. Porshia and Quency are proof of what is possible with the right state of mind.

You'll know *you're* ready to accept the challenge of the Baby Steps when you stop being an ask hole and, as they say, paint or get off the ladder, piss or get off the pot, get some grits or get out the South!

You'll also find that you've stopped caring what other people think. You stop trying to hide the process, you stop trying to make it comfortable, and you're fine with your business being out in the street. When you hit this point, you've not only entered acceptance—you've hit superhero mode. Because these days, not caring what other people think is a superpower.

You don't care if you have to ask the cashier to take something off the bill.

You don't care if someone looks over your shoulder and sees the balance in your account while you're checking it.

You don't care if someone has an annoyed look on their face every time you mention your budget.

You couldn't care less because you're in the process of rescuing your finances once and for all. You're starting to get a glimpse of yourself debt-free. You can see a glimmer of what life might look like with extra money in the bank. You have a vision for what life will look like when you're able to buy your first home.

You're changing *your* family tree. Challenge accepted.

The Lowdown

If you've made it this far, can I just stop and say how proud I am of you? The stuff we're dealing with in this book is not easy. And no one really talks about it! Up until this point, we'd sweep emotions under the rug, pretend it didn't affect us—just grin and bear it.

You were likely looking around at other folks who seemed to easily white-knuckle their way to financial freedom, thinking, *Well, dang, what's wrong with me? Why can't I do that?*

While I do think some people's personalities are more naturally bent in that direction, I believe being able to act in the midst of, or in spite of, your emotions is a skill set that anyone can develop. And now that you know what you're up against emotionally speaking, you can start to practice that skill too.

After walking through this book, I hope that you feel validated. You're *not* weird for feeling these emotions and needing to work through them—you're just human. But even more than that, I hope you feel empowered to move forward with a new knowledge of what you're truly up against as you're working the Baby Steps. Because I truly believe that awareness is half the battle! Now that you know the good and the bad of the emotions you will face, and you know the antidote to prevent or counteract any negative effects, you can continue to make progress in spite of them.

Truth be told, we've covered a ton of information so far. And it's been deep. So for your reference, there's a quick review of the basics of what we covered regarding the emotions on the next page.

If you can recognize these emotions when they start to bubble up, you can learn to work through the negative pieces of them rather than get stuck. You can keep these emotions transient, as they're meant to be, rather than camping out in them. Then you'll find you've hit the turning point: acceptance.

And hear me, you can get to acceptance no matter where you are on your money journey. Maybe you picked this book up at the very beginning of your money journey, and you still have a long while to go. You *can* get to this place of acceptance because it's simply the peaceful state where you're no longer hung up on emotions and the excuses they bring up. You're able to let those emotions pass through you as you move forward with momentum.

THE EMOTIONS OF MONEY CHEAT SHEET

Frustration: The rising sense of annoyance you feel when you believe your results don't match your efforts.

The Antidote: Do the Frustration Audit and take back your POWER.

Fear: A negative expectation of the future based on rational or irrational beliefs.

The Antidote: Focus on the fruit; the fruit is the proof. Do the Face and Replace Your Fears exercise.

Guilt: The sense of regret and fault we feel when our decisions have an unfavorable impact (real or perceived) on someone else.

Shame: The feeling that our poor decisions are our identity.

The Antidote: Find forgiveness. Embrace conviction, not condemnation. Work through the Processing Your Guilt exercise.

Anger: A passionate, retaliatory emotional response to perceived injustice.

The Antidote: Redirect anger to taking action and getting justice. Journal through the Examine Your Anger, Adjust Your Anger, Motivate Your Anger, and Embrace Thankfulness prompts.

Pity: A feeling of self-absorbed unhappiness over one's own troubles.

The Antidote: Find perspective and embrace generosity. Review the Plow Through Self-Pity checklist.

So how can you tell when you've really achieved a state of acceptance? You'll know you're here when you begin to experience what I call the Hallmarks of Acceptance.

The Hallmarks of Acceptance

You can accept the reality of your current financial situation (the good, the bad, and the ugly).

You can accept ownership for the mistakes you've made along the way.

You can accept your adverse emotions for what they are without letting them hold you back from making progress with your money.

You can accept that you've been stuck, but it's now time to move on to a more productive place.

You can accept the reality of what it'll take to work the plan and get to work.

You can accept your race as your own, not a competition against anyone else.

Reflect and Respond:

> Take some time to reflect on each hallmark, then treat them as journal prompts. Write about where you are with each of them.
>
> Have you achieved any of them? If so, which ones? Which seems to be the next logical hallmark to focus on and why?
>
> Next, write down a few of your ask hole areas. Where do you need to stop asking and finally say "Challenge accepted"?

Wow, you're getting close—I can feel it! And hey, if you need to go back to our list of emotions and antidotes, or even review a previous chapter, do it! Or even easier, just go to jadewarshaw.com/resources to get access to everything you need—including downloadable versions of the worksheets in this book as well as a link to that EveryDollar app I've been talking about. All of this will help you reach that final state of mind: acceptance. And once you're there, you're already in the winner's circle.

So when you're ready, turn the page and we'll leave that endless cycle of motion and information in the dust. It's time for action!

CHAPTER ELEVEN

IT'S TIME TO RUN

Long Train Runnin'

Signing up, training for, and running a full marathon is on my list of top three toughest, most meaningful accomplishments. The other two include giving birth to my children and, of course, paying off almost half a million dollars of debt.

Running a marathon is something I've wanted to do (in theory) for more than a decade, but there was always something that kept me from doing it. I always had a laundry list of excuses for why the current year was definitely *not* "The Year." I didn't have the time, I didn't have the fitness level, I didn't have the money, I didn't have the mental capacity, I didn't have the physical capacity, it wasn't the right time of year—you name it, I used it as a reason. As much as I liked the idea of the challenge, it also felt . . . impossible.

The truth was, I was scared. I was scared of what training for a marathon would take out of me. I had done some research, and I knew it would require around three to four months of disciplined training. Now, I've always been a fit person—I've always played sports, and I care about eating healthy. I've never shied away from a physical challenge. But this was different. This was uncharted territory. This was way outside my comfort zone.

A marathon wasn't the team sports I was used to. It wasn't me hitting the weight room and just lifting a little heavier today. And although I'd gotten into running over the years, the 26.2 miles required for a marathon was far beyond the five or six miles I was accustomed to. Still, something was calling me toward it.

I'd talked about trying a marathon since 2012—and twelve years later, I decided to answer the call. All the reasons *not to* were still there. Actually, now there were more reasons: now I was forty years old, now I had two children, now I had a new job with different time demands, and now I would be training alone instead of with Sam, thanks to crazy schedules. But it was now or never. I realized there would never be a perfect time. And if I was being honest, if there had ever *been* a perfect time, those days were likely behind me—when I was younger, childless, and had more free time on my hands.

But those days were gone, and if I didn't make my move, I knew there would come a time where it was too late. I knew deep inside that if I didn't take the opportunity to push myself, to see what I was truly made of, I'd regret it. So I decided to run.

Pastor David Hughes once told me, "Preparation is a gift you give yourself." If there ever was a time when that bit of wisdom stuck with me, it was at this time. The race was in October, so I started preparing in August. The training included four runs each week, with times and mileage gradually increasing over time. I viewed staying committed to the training schedule and not missing any days as a gift I was giving myself because, come race day, flaking out on training wouldn't hurt anyone but me. If I was going to do the race, I had to accept the plan for what it was and fully commit. My goal was to run the entire 26.2 miles without walking.

Let me tell you, the training was a roller coaster. Some days were a breeze; other days I was running six miles in the pouring rain or struggling to not pass out under the summer sun. Then there were days where external factors were just fine but internally I was fighting the fight of my life. It was a mental feat just to roll out of bed before the sun was up, lace up my shoes, and put one foot in front of the other. Over those months I battled hip pain, IT band issues, chafing, and a strained hamstring. But I just kept reminding myself, *Jade, you knew it wouldn't be easy. The time is going to pass anyway, and when October comes, you will either be a champion, or you will have given up. Accept the challenge!*

Staying committed for the whole journey meant that I needed to come up with systems to reinforce my training habits. I laid my running clothes out, filled up my water bottles, and put my electrolytes on the counter the night before, so it was all ready for me in the morning. I had my breakfast planned out, so I knew what to eat. I also planned for things to keep me motivated. I had a list of audiobooks that I was excited to listen to, and I had two different running playlists that gave me the eye of the tiger. And on the days of my longest runs, I planned a great reward. I got to eat my favorite food: nachos. Last but not least, I made sure plenty of people knew that I was training for the race—I needed the accountability.

It also didn't take long to realize that being prepped with a few simple tools could make a big difference when it came to some of the more challenging conditions I was dealing with. I invested in a couple of great pairs of running shoes to help keep my form and joints intact. On those hot days, I used a waterproof SPF face lotion to protect my skin. (I'm not trying to age any faster than necessary!) A water belt came in clutch to keep me hydrated. And when I struggled with chafing—it's *diabolical* what fabric rubbing against your skin for hours on end can do—I found a chafing stick ASAP to help with the friction.

The final tool was a gift Sam bought me. It was a pair of Oakley reflector sunglasses. They had white frames with rainbow iridescent fuchsia and orange lenses. Truthfully, they looked like something Macho Man Randy Savage would have worn. So at first, I was reluctant. (Listen, I love the '90s. I even enjoy wrestling. But even I have my limits.) But this wasn't just a tool to protect my eyes as I ran for hours in the bright Tennessee sun—it was more than that. As Sam handed the glasses to me, he said, "I bought a pair for myself too, and I noticed that when I put them on, I transform into someone else. The moment I put these sunglasses on, I become a marathoner." And they did the same for me. Turns out the right tools don't only help you stay consistent; they can help you transform.

Having those built-in systems and the right tools to help when I needed them was critical for my success. And when race day finally came, I had a crazy realization: The hard part was already done.

The challenge wasn't the final race. (I knew how to run!) Committing to the journey was the hard part. Showing up each day was the battle. Putting in the work and sacrificing each day, knowing there were still weeks and weeks in front of me of the same grind, was the challenge. The day it was time to run 26.2 miles was actually the easiest day. I knew I would finish the race. I'd already accepted the challenge. I'd taken ownership of my training and preparation, and today I was just running out the final action steps. I had full confidence. At that point, victory was inevitable.

On October 22, 2024, Sam and I completed our first marathon—and I met my goal to run the entire time. At the end of the race, Sam and I laid there in the grass field at the finish line, just staring at each other, salt and sweat streaming down our faces, our bodies weak and muscles trembling from the work. As we stared at each other, our eyes filled with tears. In that moment, we were both feeling the same thing. This wasn't the first marathon we'd run, but the second.

The first marathon we'd run together was from January of 2008 to October 2017—our race to pay off every cent of our $460,066.56 of debt. The parallels were uncanny. And in that moment, it was a joy to experience that victory together for a second time. We learned that when you accept the challenge to push yourself, you will find that you are more powerful than you ever imagined, and you can accomplish things you once thought were impossible.

Minute by Minute

Here's the truth: We wouldn't have been successful if we'd let our emotions stop us.

The moment I accepted that the training was necessary, that it was a gift of preparation I could give myself, I was able to take ownership of my actions, follow through, and stay disciplined. The more I trained, the more confident I became that I could finish. One by one, all the excuses I'd started with began fading into the distance. Running across the finish line was the only thing in sight.

Walking the Baby Steps is the same way. There will never be a perfect time to start. The list of reasons *not to* commit will always be there. And truthfully, the longer you wait, the more that list could grow—a new baby, a new job, a new move, a new relationship. But there will come a day where it may be too late to accomplish all that you could today. Don't get me wrong, no matter your situation, there is always a greater measure of peace that can be obtained. But if at all possible, I want you to experience the fullness of the Baby Steps, which means today is a great day to start.

The Baby Steps are a marathon, and truthfully, the first three Baby Steps feel like an all-out sprint. Your body feels it, your heart feels it, and your emotions definitely feel it. You will be pushed to the limit, and there will be moments you want to quit. There will be days when it feels like everything is stacked against you. There will be days that a bill comes in the mail out of the blue and sets you back by weeks. There could be unforeseen job losses, medical bills, relationship challenges—you name it.

But if you keep going, there are also really great moments—the moments you keep promises to yourself and realize you are capable of doing what you say you'll do. And when you cross the finish line and your debt is gone . . . when you have four months of savings for the first time in your life . . . when you can sleep at night with financial stability and peace . . . trust me, you won't be sorry.

It Keeps You Runnin'

Once you've accepted the challenge of the Baby Steps, setting yourself up for success is crucial. Just like with a marathon, you'll need the right systems in place and the right tools in your belt to help keep you motivated, accountable, and rewarded until you cross the finish line. Being extra-intentional—like I was in laying out workout clothes and preplanning meals—will make it easier for you to keep your commitments. And much like those Macho Man sunglasses, using the proper tools can help you transform into a money "marathoner."

So, let's talk about five areas you can focus on with the right systems and tools.

1. Daily Habits

In the grand scheme of things, everything boils down to daily habits. Sam and I got ourselves into debt one decision at a time, and that's how we got out. The same will be true for you. And doing a few practical things will help you show up the way you need to for your money journey.

First, just like I said way back in chapter 2, you need to start with a written budget. Once you have that, you can put systems in place to make sure you're sticking to it. Set an alarm on your phone to remind you to check in on your budget every day and track your transactions—every transaction. You can do all this on paper, but I will always recommend downloading the Every-Dollar app to make this as simple as possible. This thing is the most practical tool in your arsenal—the chafing stick of money management, if you will. You don't have to do the math or check your account. It does it all for you, taking all the friction out of doing your budget, so you have literally no excuse. And that's key because keeping the current state of your money in the forefront of your mind will help you stay on task.

To keep your spending tight, you can also try pulling out cash for certain purchases and utilizing the Envelope System. This is where you set aside actual cash in physical envelopes for specific budget categories. When the cash is gone, you're done spending in that category for the month. And look, cash is magical because you feel it when you spend it. Electronic purchase methods and plastic cards don't have the same impact on our brain as cash does—there isn't enough friction for us to *feel* the fact that our hard-earned money is leaving our account. So if you need a daily habit to keep your spending in check, try using cash for things like groceries and restaurants.

Speaking of food, it's a fact: Food is most people's biggest budget buster. Whether it's restaurants, DoorDash, or picking up drive-thru, how much we spend on food is a problem. So simple changes like packing your lunch the night before and meal planning for the week are also great habits you can develop that your future self will thank you for. They come in clutch when you're feeling tempted to get off track.

And finally, there's a really great way to set yourself up to win, and it's on your phone. Well, technically, it's taking something *off* your phone. It's time to delete the apps that tempt you to spend—shopping apps (yes, even Amazon), gaming apps, sports betting, all of it! You heard me: If it tempts you to spend money, it's got to go! And while you're at it, unsubscribe from all those emails from Wayfair, Fashion Nova, Lululemon, and whatever other retailers are blowing up your inbox with the latest deals.

2. Daily Motivation

I think the number-one question I get asked is this: How do I stay motivated? First and foremost, I believe motivation comes through awareness. It's the result of being aware of wins, big and small. That starts with being able to see progress and feel the support that keeps you running, that helps you keep moving and build momentum. And a big part of that can come from the daily habits we just talked about. When you do those daily habits, they create awareness. You're able to look back on your day or your week and see, *Here are the ways I've won.*

I can see I've stuck to my budget.
I can see I've brought my lunch every day.

I notice the positive effects of meal planning on my spending.

I haven't opened the Amazon app in weeks.

Another great way to see the progress you're making is to simply write it down in a journal. When you stop and document everything in a journal, you're keeping clear records of starting points, struggles, and progress made. If you're not the writing type, you can use those debt and payment trackers that you can color in as you go. The point here is to create a clear visual of your accomplishments. Each small win is a little dopamine hit when you realize, *Yes! I did good right there!* That feedback loop is important to experience, and it entices us to want to keep going.

When I was training for the marathon, I used an app that tracked each run. Being able to see all my runs in one spot was motivating for me to continue. Being able to see that I'd started at three miles and now I was running *fifteen* got me pumped! The same is true with your money. Whether it's taking a screenshot of your balance each time you pay down the debt or texting your best friend each time you add more to your savings, create a ritual of record keeping.

Another important part of motivation is found in a community of like-minded people. I mentioned before that listening to *The Ramsey Show* was inspiring to Sam and me because we heard stories of people just like us who were running the same race. You need that community. It's like the energy goo packs you eat throughout a race to help you keep going when you're losing steam.

When I showed up to run the marathon, there were thousands of other folks who had gone through their version of the same journey. There was even one guy who looked to be in his late sixties running faster than me. Now seeing *that* was motivating! That was the pep in my step I needed! And in this case, you can use the exact same "energy goo" Sam and I did—we're just two of millions of people who have relied on *The Ramsey Show* content, and seeing others win with money helped us stay motivated in our money marathon.

But it's not just about seeing—we have to feel it too. Finding community by taking or teaching classes like Financial Peace University or signing up for a group coaching session are all not only great tools, they're also great ways that real people can intersect our lives and remind us that we're not alone. Feeling the support of other folks running alongside us is critical to staying motivated.

3. Regular Rewards

When it comes to completing any race, milestones matter because milestones signal that it's time to celebrate. Money milestones are no different and are an important system to implement. Look at your situation, map out ahead of time what your milestones will be, and then create a reasonable way to celebrate and reward your efforts.

The rewards are not intended to throw you off track. Rewards are a tool to signal success. After my long runs, I had a plate of nachos and a margarita—I didn't go on a twenty-four-hour bender of nacho cheese and bottomless tequila. Obviously, that would be detrimental to my training.

The same is true when it comes time to celebrate your money milestones. I find this practice to be particularly important during Baby Step 2. Now you likely won't be in it for seven and a half years like Sam and I were, but I'd say that if you're in it for more than a year, you need to figure out some milestones to celebrate. It could be as simple as ordering a pizza from your favorite spot and making a pan of brownies when you hit three months of sticking to your budget and meal plan.

Or for a bigger milestone like paying off $25,000, the kids go to the grandparents' house and you get a hotel room downtown and enjoy an adult night out. In our case, when we hit four years of working the plan, Sam and I said, "No more air mattress. We're buying a new bedframe and mattress in cash."

Planning for the milestone rewards is a type of positive reinforcement. You're working hard for a long period of time—you need some moments of celebration in there. Milestones also keep you in control, as opposed to feeling like the plan is controlling you. You get to decide what and when to celebrate, so it keeps the experience rewarding.

4. Accountability

When I made the decision to run the marathon, I told folks about it! I wanted people to know so they could ask me about it and I'd have to be accountable. But also, since Sam and I agreed to do the race together, I had built-in accountability, which was a key system for sticking to my part and doing the training.

Money is the same way. When we were first walking the Baby Steps, I wish we had told more people we trust early on. We made the mistake of isolating ourselves, and I don't want to see you do the same. Making sure you have trusted people in your corner to hold you to your work is the move.

I once read that Oprah Winfrey, on a quest to slim down, hired someone to literally slap the food out of her hand whenever she was about to eat something unhealthy. Who knows whether that's true or just an urban legend? But what I do know is that you need to get around people who have done what you want to do, who are doing what you want to do, who believe in what you are trying to do—and therefore have the clout to hold you responsible. That's what Quency and Porshia did, and that accountability led to winning.

You're looking for people who share your beliefs and will offer accountability. These are the people who will encourage you, cheer for you, and, when necessary, tell you when you're trippin'. These people are truth tellers, and they'll make you feel irritated and stretched sometimes because they know what you are capable of, and they want to see you succeed because they believe you *can* do what you said you would do. These are the people who will slap the credit card out of your hand and smile in your face while they do it. These are the folks who will look you up and down and say, "Those new shoes? I thought you said you weren't spending money on the clothes this month. Call me when you take them back." These are real ones. And you need them in your life.

But if you're thinking, *Jade, I don't have anyone like that!* or if you just need an accountability partner with more financial expertise, there's an amazing tool out there—and I don't even have to use a metaphor for this one: a coach. Just like having your own personal marathon training coach, you can find a personal finance coach who will help you stick to the plan you've committed to, especially if you're having a tougher time navigating your path. And I get it—your people can't be with you every single moment of the day to hold you accountable. But I know that phone is, and on top of being a great budgeting tool, the EveryDollar app also has some incredible tools inside to help with daily habits, motivation, accountability, and guidance. It's the perfect tool to walk with you through your money emotions. It will teach you, challenge your beliefs, and give you step-by-step actions to complete every day to make sure you make the most of your money.

It's honestly like a personal finance coach in your pocket. It has everything you need to keep you running all the way to the finish line. Today it's the only budget I use—and I wish Sam and I had this back when our journey first started. It would've saved us a lot of time, energy, and arguments! Scan the QR code at the end of this book today to get started with EveryDollar and make accountability automatic every step of the way.

5. Mental Check-Ins

I know we've talked about some deep things in this book. Although throughout these pages I've compared what you're going through to a fight, a race, a journey, a movie, a song, and other things to make the connection, I want you to know I also see it for exactly what it is. Tough stuff. Deep stuff.

Quiet time or solitude was a system I put into place early on to keep my head on straight. You'll want to find out what this looks like for you. For me, this often took the form of a run or a walk—or I'd wake up early and have quiet time to clear my head and check in with myself mentally and spiritually before I started my day.

For some of us, the emotional depths will be tougher to navigate, and we'll need to enlist professional help. I fully support this decision. And my buddy Dr. John Delony can help. He's a mental-health expert and master counselor who offers guidance on relationships, anxiety, and wellness. Dr. John can guide and connect you with even more tools and resources to find emotional healing and wellness.

When I was training for the marathon, my health was the most powerful tool I had. It's hard to run when you aren't physically healthy. And the same is true with money. The truth is, it hard to run when you aren't healthy mentally or relationally. A good counselor might end up being the most powerful tool you use.

What a Fool Believes

In the midst of all this good energy, I feel the need to give a fair warning. When you enter acceptance and start taking action, you will be foolish to think that you are simply signing up for a financial challenge. As a matter of fact, that couldn't be further from the truth. The changes and transformation that take place as a result of you accepting the Baby Steps journey cannot and should not be compartmentalized to just your bank account.

Just before Sam and I signed up for the race, a friend of Sam's who had run a marathon a few months earlier told him, in fair warning, "Get ready, man, because this race really starts to take over your whole life."

I thought he just meant timewise. But boy, was I wrong. That race did start to take over my life. It impacted my meal choices, my sleep schedule, my work schedule, my days off, and what shoes I could or couldn't wear. I had to adjust my budget for shoes and gear—and it changed how my clothes fit. I constantly had to be aware of how much water I had. I had to wash my hair three times as often as usual. I became obsessed with staying healthy so I *could* run.

Those things were all directly or indirectly related to the race. But then I noticed things taking place that had nothing to do with the race. When I started training, it was during one of the toughest seasons in my life I've had in a while. I was going through a really down time in life, feeling lost and lonely, and I needed something to focus on. Because of the training, I had these long stretches of time—and so I had more time to talk to God. I prayed a lot and found the clarity that I was looking for in areas of my life that had absolutely nothing to do with the marathon. I ended up with patience and perseverance to not only run the physical race in front of me but run the race that life in general was presenting me.

The same thing happens on the money front. Getting your money in a healthy place feeds into your relationships—especially if you're married. It will likely push you to work through boundary issues with your parents or in-laws, or communication issues with your spouse. For me, it crept into my spiritual life. I was like, "God, I need help!" I found myself more tuned in to my spiritual life than ever before. Of course, my physical body was impacted. I've said it before, and I'll say it again: Being on a budget isn't an excuse to eat crap like ramen and fast food to save money. For me, it was the opposite. In order to save money, I was meal planning and cooking from scratch—and eating healthier than ever.

And since we weren't spending a lot of money on entertainment, Sam and I went for walks or exercised as a way to spend quality time together. I'm telling you; this money thing is contagious—the effects spread like crazy! When you get healthy in one area of your life, the other areas begin to demand it as well. It's an awareness that sets in, and suddenly you're motivated to create consistency, boundaries, and discipline in other areas as well. This journey is the real deal. It's real transformation. Your heart, mind, habits, and emotions change. And that can be a lot to deal with.

After the marathon, none of my clothes fit the same, my hamstring was tender, my endurance was better than ever, and my metabolism was incredible. I was still experiencing the effects of the race weeks after it was over. After walking Baby Steps 1 through 5, I continued to feel the effects too—really amazing ones, like the continued freedom of not having debt, the peace of having six months of savings, the ease of spending without guilt, the security of having money in retirement . . . The list goes on and on.

But there were also a few confusing side effects I didn't expect. Back in the fall of 2022, when our family moved to Tennessee for my new career at Ramsey Solutions, I noticed something really strange. I was just a mess of emotions ready to fire at any moment, and I didn't know what was causing it. So I decided to go to counseling.

Waiting to Exhale

I sat on the other end of the Zoom call, staring at my counselor—completely stumped.

"Doc, I don't know what's up with me," I finally said. "I'm crying at the drop of the hat. Everything gets me choked up. I can't work like this! I'm in the best place I've been with my marriage, with my career, with our money. I feel like God and I are vibing, and yet my emotions are wilding out. Help me out, what's going on?"

She took a deep breath.

"Could it be that you're *not* running anymore?" she asked. "Could it be that, for the first time, you are safe, and you feel secure? For the first time, you're experiencing true stability? And because you're finally experiencing this peace financially, your heart and mind feel that it's safe for you to release the other areas it was holding back. Areas where you don't have the same peace and freedom."

I was shook.

It turns out, being in that healthy place of freedom financially was requiring that I find freedom in other places in my heart, mind, and past. Places that had nothing to do with my wallet. It was a watershed moment. I'd never considered this. I'd been waiting to exhale for so long—and now it was here. My body was . . . exhaling. I'd let the financial struggles go, and my body was ready to let go of all the other struggles right along with it. For the next six months, she and I talked through all of it, and I let emotions go that I hadn't even realized I'd been harboring.

Dr. John Delony talks all the time about *our body* feeling the weight of our debts and money stress. And it's so, so true. Our bodies feel the risk we're in, whether we're leveraged up to our eyeballs flipping properties or working at the drugstore barely living paycheck-to-paycheck. Our body knows when we aren't safe, when we can't breathe. And then, of course, our body takes measures to try to protect us by building up whatever walls and safety measures to keep everything tied up tight. In my case, I was someone who had to keep it all together all the time. I didn't have the time or space to cry or deal with anything other than our money situation.

But once we do find that security, it's like when you reach cruising altitude on an airplane and the captain turns off the fasten seat-belt sign. It's necessary to reach that altitude where all signs point to a safe ride. Then we realize we can take off the restraints tying us down, and we can finally stretch out; we're free to go about the rest of the cabin.

We can move. We can breathe. We can be free.

See, one thing I've learned is that freedom begets freedom. Freedom wants to be all-encompassing. It's doesn't want to be cooped up or compartmentalized. And when you think about it, that's the very definition of the word *freedom*: without hindrance or restraint. The concept makes me think of that familiar promise in Scripture: Who the Son sets free, is free indeed. Free completely.

So just a fair warning, friend to friend: When you accept the Baby Steps and the freedom they help you achieve, be prepared for it to seep into the most important areas of your life. For me, it turned out that finding financial peace wasn't just *financial*—it was Jade peace. It wasn't just *financial* freedom—it was Jade freedom.

And I believe it's the same for you. That's why it's such a fight. That's why it's such a struggle. But I promise, it's worth it.

I said it in chapter 1 but want to say it again here, so you can see what that freedom looks like.

- Where there was once frustration, you will feel confident and understand the virtue of patience.
- Where you were once racked with guilt and shame, you will feel unapologetic and bold.
- Where you once felt fear, you will feel safe and secure—possibly for the first time ever—eager to embrace change and opportunity.
- Where there was once pity, you'll feel opportunity. You'll be filled with hope and new perspective.
- And where you were once so angry, you'll finally feel peace. You won't need that old anger anymore.

Then, you will stand in acceptance. Accepting that you committed to do a hard thing and you can complete it. Accepting that your emotions may present obstacles, but you can overcome them. And finally, accepting the peace and freedom you will have run so hard to achieve. And then, when your race is complete, you'll finally have the chance to exhale. You'll finally be free.

But for today? Today, it's time to run. You know what you're up against emotionally and tactically—and now you have the tools and strategies and systems to keep running. You officially have every single thing you need to cross the finish line. Trust me, you're ready.

CONCLUSION

Forget Me Nots

I want to tell you that I'm so very proud of you. What you're embarking on is not easy. Few even consider the changes you're about to go through. It may not be easy, but now you have everything you need to finish this race strong.

I want to tell you that I believe in you. I see you as so very powerful and so very capable. If I didn't think you could do this, I wouldn't have written this book. But you can—so I did. You've got this! I don't care what caused you to stop before. The finish line is still there, and this time you're gonna make it across.

I want to tell you that you are a marvel. You are being pulled toward this process because you, my friend, are a boss. You are a hero. You understand the assignment, and you can be trusted to get the job done.

I want to tell you that you are a force. The choices you make next will have a ripple effect that's hard to fathom. Freedom is never just about you. When you make the choice to run this race, you've officially become a trailblazer. There are a lot of dominos—what an honor to be called as the first one in your line to tip and fall in the right direction.

I want to tell you—it's not just about you.

I've said it before, and I'll say it again. Freedom begets freedom. Peace begets peace. You have something inside of you that someone else needs too. It's not just for you. It's for your family—your spouse, your kids, your nieces and nephews. It's for folks you've yet to meet. And before you close this book, I want to leave you with these words from Marianne Williamson.

> Our deepest fear is not that we are inadequate, our deepest fear is that we are powerful beyond measure. It is our light, not our darkness that most frightens us. . . . You are a child of God. Your playing small does not serve the world. There is nothing enlightened about shrinking so that other people won't feel insecure around you. We are all meant to shine, as children do. . . . It's not just in some of us; it's in everyone. And as we let our own light shine, we unconsciously give other people permission to do the same. As we are liberated from our own fear, our presence automatically liberates others.[22]

Freedom and liberation are in your reach, so *don't give up*.

Rip out this page, and tape it on your mirror.

It's time to do this.

YOUR CHALLENGE, SHOULD YOU CHOOSE TO ACCEPT IT

(And you should. Otherwise, why did you read this whole book?)

This is your moment—I want you to scan the QR code and download the EveryDollar app. This will be the single most important tool you will use on your financial journey. Because it's not just the best budgeting app out there. It's the app that gives you personalized recommendations on how to free up more margin and make real progress. Every single day. It's basically like having me in your pocket, telling you exactly what to do next based on *your* situation. And trust me, it works. The average user finds *thousands* of dollars they didn't know they had just on the first day. That's incredible!

But like I've been saying, it's not just about the money. It's about staying the course when your emotions try to lead you astray. Having that digital coach by your side to show you the next right step will be just what you need to make the most of your valuable time and effort—so you can finally win with money and finally be free! And in the spirit of freedom, I'm giving you a free trial of EveryDollar so you can try it for yourself. So go ahead—scan the QR code and get your head start!

See you at the finish line.

ACKNOWLEDGMENTS

Okay, so here's an embarrassing story. One day back in 2007, I was bored and said to myself, *I'd like to be a writer—I think I'll try to write a book*. I scratched out two paragraphs about the importance of finding purpose in your life . . . and quickly realized it sucked. I had nothing to say. I hadn't really lived much adult life yet. I still have those two paragraphs saved on a thumb drive, and I've thought about them so many times as I wrote this book.

First, I guess it really happened. Look, Mom! I'm a writer! Second, who knew purpose would be the underlying driver? There is a purpose for everything we go through, and in my case, yeah, part of that meant writing a book about it. Third, no one just "sits down to write a book." It takes a lot of talented people to make it happen. Ergo, my deepest thanks to . . .

Him who is able to do exceedingly, abundantly above all that we ask or think, according to the power that works in us. To you, Lord, I give praise. Thanks for the endurance. Thanks for the ideas. Thanks for the grace. Thanks for surrounding me with the right folks.

My family—Sam and my beautiful kiddos—for your patience while I was holed up in my office, for understanding all the times I said, "five more minutes" (which really meant "another hour or so"), and for enduring my scattered listening skills for six months, knowing part of my brain was always preoccupied with something book related. I'm so blessed to have you as my family, my own personal people. Thank you for allowing me to do this. I love you.

Dave Ramsey, for sharing. You shared your story, you shared your solutions, and then you shared the platform. I don't know if I'll ever quite fully grasp that. It could've been anyone. Thanks for sharing with me and the other Personalities. My hope is that by listening to you and getting to sit next to you, some of what you are has gotten on me and, I hope, will show in this book.

Pastor David Hughes, for being the guide, for being my pastor and my friend. I've hidden so many of your words in my heart, and so much of what you've taught me over the years poured onto the page. Thank you.

Amy Severson, for being the first person to hear Sam's and my story and champion it. I'm forever grateful to you. Thank you, thank you, thank you!

Katie Crenshaw, the *big* homie. I won't be able to get it on the page, so how can I put this? You're the reason we got as far as a book! In the latter part of 2023 and for most of 2024, I needed someone to hold me down—and you did that. I truly thank God for you. You didn't let me give up. Thank you.

Preston Cannon, oh captain, my captain! Thanks for leading me through this crazy process, steering me in the right direction, and keeping us on course. You've always encouraged me to be my full self. We may never see eye to eye on Phil Collins, but you are one of my favorite folks to work with because you always keep it 100. Thank you for all of it.

Mary-Kate Tucto, my editor. What a human being. It takes a lot of . . . well, everything to work with me. And you had what it takes and more. It was a privilege to push and pull with you and end up exactly where we landed with this book. Thank you—you are so very talented, so full of wonderful ideas, and a masterful problem solver. I have nothing but the utmost respect for you!

Rick Prall, for helping me outline this beast. Thank you so much! "What a time it is for us to be alive!"

Caitlyn Cantabrana, for being the best administrative assistant in the world. Thank you for guarding my calendar with your life and keeping me on task and on deadline.

Jeremy Breland and Daniel Ramsey, for your encouraging words in the early phases of this manuscript. Thanks for cheering this work on!

Kris Evans, Chris Campbell, Brian Hamilton, Power Jensen, and the entire EveryDollar crew, for partnering with me. You guys are rock stars!

Creatives extraordinaire Brad Dennison, Kyle Hofmann, Seth Farmer, and Riley Clark, for your work making this book beautiful.

Nick Ahrens, Alex Hearn, Will Smith, Savannah Pickens, Hailey Lance, and Wes Freitas, for your brainstorming efforts.

Brian Horvath, for getting this thing in stores and on shelves. Along with Kate Flynn, Nikia Wade, Ragan Fletcher, Luke Bierly, Laura Kooistra, Jackie Page, and all the marketing magicians who will get this book into people's hands and lives.

Taylor Griffin, Samantha Ellis, and the rest of the PR Team, for helping get the word out on the street.

The audiobook genius of Kelly Daniel and Paul Salveson, for allowing people like me to live in their strength by listening instead of reading.

My good friends Lucas Gomes, Rob Lopez, Porshia Gordon, and Quency Gordon, the most creative people I know. Thanks for letting me bounce ideas off you and for all your creative insights.

My fellow Ramsey Personalities—George, Eddie, John, Rachel, my dawg Ken Coleman, and the OG, Dave Ramsey. I still can't believe I get to work alongside you giants. May the privilege of what we get to do never be lost on us.

My Church By The Glades family. You know who you are. You are my family. You are my home. It's rare air—and if you breathe it in, it *will* change you.

The Hughes, Palacios, Evans, and Uhl families, for always, always pouring.

NOTES

1. "Median Weekly Earnings of Full-Time Workers Were $1,145 in the Fourth Quarter of 2023," *The Economics Daily*, U.S. Bureau of Labor Statistics, January 25, 2024, https://www.bls.gov/opub/ted/2024/median-weekly-earnings-of-full-time-workers-were-1145-in-the-fourth-quarter-of-2023.htm.
2. "Quarterly Report on Household Debt and Credit: Q1 2025," Federal Reserve Bank of New York, May 2025, https://www.newyorkfed.org/medialibrary/interactives/householdcredit/data/pdf/HHDC_2025Q1.
3. "State of the Automotive Finance Market: Q1 2024," Experian, https://www.experian.com/content/dam/noindex/na/us/automotive/finance-trends/2024/experian-safm-q1-2024.pdf; Martin Dasko, "More Than 40% of Americans Have Car Payments: Here's How Much They're Paying," *GOBankingRates*, November 8, 2023, https://www.gobankingrates.com/saving-money/car/over-40-percent-have-car-payments-heres-how-much-theyre-paying/.
4. Hannah Gdalman, MK Falgout, Necati Celik, and Meghan Greene, *FinHealth Spend Report 2024*, Financial Health Network, August 2024, https://finhealthnetwork.org/wp-content/uploads/2024/08/FinHealth-Spend-Report-2024-FHN.pdf.
5. "The State of Personal Finance Q2 2023," Ramsey Solutions, August 2023, https://www.ramseysolutions.com/budgeting/state-of-personal-finance.

6. 2023 "Getting Paid In America" Survey Results, PayrollOrg, September 2023, https://info.payroll.org/pdfs/npw/2023_Getting_Paid_In_America_survey_results.pdf.
7. "INTOO Layoff Anxiety Study," INTOO and The Harris Poll, June 2019, https://resources.intoo.com/guides/layoff-anxiety-study.
8. Johanna Maleh and Tiffany Bosley, *Disability and Death Probability Tables for Insured Workers Who Attain Age 20 in 2023,* Actuarial Note No. 2023.6, Social Security Administration, July 2023, https://www.ssa.gov/oact/NOTES/ran6/an2023-6.pdf.
9. "The State of Personal Finance Q1 2025," Ramsey Solutions, May 1, 2025, https://www.ramseysolutions.com/budgeting/state-of-personal-finance.
10. "The Financial Literacy Crisis in America: 2023 Report," Ramsey Solutions, December 15, 2023, https://www.ramseysolutions.com/financial-literacy/financial-literacy-crisis-in-america.
11. "Financial Literacy Crisis: 2023 Report," Ramsey Solutions.
12. Jasmine Escalera, "4 out of 5 Workers Fear Job Loss in 2025: The Great Stay Explained," MyPerfectResume, January 21, 2025, https://www.myperfectresume.com/career-center/careers/the-great-stay.
13. "State of Personal Finance Q1 2025," Ramsey Solutions.
14. 2023 "Getting Paid In America" Survey Results, PayrollOrg.
15. "Changes in U.S. Family Finances from 2017 to 2019: Evidence from the Survey of Consumer Finances," Federal Reserve, September 2020, https://www.federalreserve.gov/publications/files/scf20.pdf.
16. "State of Personal Finance Q1 2025," Ramsey Solutions.
17. Mark Hyman, MD (@drmarkhyman), Instagram, December 8, 2024, https://www.instagram.com/drmarkhyman/p/DDUlJXtPFar/.
18. Chris Voss with Tahl Raz, *Never Split the Difference: Negotiating as If Your Life Depended on It* (New York, NY: Harper Business, 2016), 96–112.

19. "What's in my FICO scores?," *myFICO*, accessed May 19, 2025, https://www.myfico.com/credit-education/whats-in-your-credit-score.
20. Katherine Johnson, "What Matters – Katherine Johnson: NASA Pioneer and 'Computer,'" WHRO Public Media, February 25, 2011, YouTube video, 26:03, https://www.youtube.com/watch?v=r8gJqKyIGhE.
21. James Clear, *Atomic Habits: An Easy & Proven Way to Build Good Habits & Break Bad Ones* (New York, NY: Avery, 2018), 141–43.
22. Marianne Williamson, *A Return to Love: Reflections on the Principles of "A Course in Miracles"* (New York, NY: HarperCollins, 1996), 190.